OLIVER TWIST

When *Oliver Twist* was first published in 1838, it was not fashionable to write novels that showed life in all its miserable reality. But Dickens wanted to shock his readers. He wanted to show criminals as they really were, and to reveal all the horrors and violence that hid in the narrow, dirty backstreets of London. So he gives us the evil Fagin, the brutal Bill Sikes, and a crowd of thieves and robbers, who lie and cheat and steal, and live in fear of prison or the hangman's rope around their necks.

Dickens also had another purpose. He wanted to show that goodness can survive through every kind of hardship. So he gives us little Oliver Twist – an orphan thrown into a world of poverty and crime, starved and beaten and unloved. He gives us Nancy – poor, miserable, unhappy Nancy, who struggles to stay loyal in a cruel world.

And, as in all the best stories, goodness triumphs over evil in the end.

OXFORD BOOKWORMS LIBRARY
Classics

Oliver Twist

Stage 6 (2500 headwords)

Series Editor: Jennifer Bassett
Founder Editor: Tricia Hedge
Activities Editors: Jennifer Bassett and Alison Baxter

CHARLES DICKENS

Oliver Twist

Retold by
Richard Rogers

OXFORD UNIVERSITY PRESS

OXFORD
UNIVERSITY PRESS

Great Clarendon Street, Oxford OX2 6DP

Oxford University Press is a department of the University of Oxford.
It furthers the University's objective of excellence in research, scholarship,
and education by publishing worldwide in

Oxford New York

Auckland Bangkok Buenos Aires Cape Town Chennai
Dar es Salaam Delhi Hong Kong Istanbul Karachi Kolkata
Kuala Lumpur Madrid Melbourne Mexico City Mumbai
Nairobi São Paulo Shanghai Taipei Tokyo Toronto

OXFORD and OXFORD ENGLISH are registered trade marks of
Oxford University Press in the UK and in certain other countries

© Oxford University Press 2000

Database right Oxford University Press (maker)

First published in Oxford Bookworms 1992
8 10 12 14 16 15 13 11 9 7

ISBN 0 19 423092 9

A complete recording of this Bookworms edition of
Oliver Twist is available on cassette ISBN 0 19 422889 4

Printed in Spain by Unigraf S.L.

Illustrations by: George Cruikshank
from the engravings in the 1946 edition

CONTENTS

PEOPLE IN THIS STORY

Oliver Twist

Mrs Mann, *in charge of the 'baby farm'*

Mr Bumble, *the beadle*

Mrs Corney, *a widow, in charge of the workhouse*

Old Sally, *a woman in the workhouse*

Mr Sowerberry, *an undertaker*

Mrs Sowerberry, *his wife*

Charlotte, *the Sowerberrys' servant*

Noah Claypole, *a charity-boy*

Fagin

The Artful Dodger ⎫
⎬ *Fagin's boys*
Charley Bates ⎭

Bill Sikes, *a robber*

Nancy, *Bill Sikes' girl*

Monks, *a mysterious stranger*

Mr Brownlow, *an old gentleman*

Mrs Bedwin, *Mr Brownlow's housekeeper*

Mr Grimwig, *an old friend of Mr Brownlow's*

Mrs Maylie, *a kind lady*

Harry Maylie, *her son*

Rose Maylie, *her niece*

Dr Losberne, *a friend of the Maylies'*

1
Oliver's early life

Oliver Twist was born in a workhouse, and when he arrived in this hard world, it was very doubtful whether he would live beyond the first three minutes. He lay on a hard little bed and struggled to start breathing.

Oliver fought his first battle without much assistance from the two people present at his birth. One was an old woman, who was nearly always drunk, and the other was a busy local doctor, who was not paid enough to be very interested in Oliver's survival. After all, death was a common event in the workhouse, where only the poor and homeless lived.

However, Oliver managed to draw his first breath, and then announced his arrival to the rest of the workhouse by crying loudly. His mother raised her pale young face from the pillow and whispered, 'Let me see the child, and die.'

The doctor turned away from the fire, where he had been warming his hands. 'You must not talk about dying yet,' he said to her kindly. He gave her the child to hold. Lovingly, she kissed the baby on its forehead with her cold white lips, then stared wildly around the room, fell back – and died.

'Poor dear!' said the nurse, hurriedly putting a green glass bottle back in the pocket of her long skirt.

The doctor began to put on his coat. 'The baby is weak and will probably have difficulties,' he said. 'If so, give it a little milk to keep it quiet.' Then he looked at the dead woman. 'The mother was a good-looking girl. Where did she come from?'

'She was brought here last night,' replied the old woman. 'She

1

was found lying in the street. She'd walked some distance, judging by her shoes, which were worn to pieces. Where she came from, where she was going to, or what her name was, nobody knows.'

The doctor lifted the girl's left hand. 'The old story,' he said sadly, shaking his head. 'No wedding ring, I see. Ah! Good night.'

And so Oliver was left with only the drunken nurse. Without clothes, under his first blanket, he could have been the child of a king or a beggar. But when the woman dressed him later in rough cotton clothes, yellow with age, he looked exactly what he was – an orphan in a workhouse, ready for a life of misery, hunger, and neglect.

Oliver cried loudly. If he could have known that he was a workhouse orphan, perhaps he would have cried even more loudly.

There was no one to look after the baby in the workhouse, so Oliver was sent to a special 'baby farm' nearby. There, he and thirty other children rolled around the floor all day, without the inconvenience of too much food or too much clothing. Mrs Mann, the old woman who 'looked after' them, was very experienced. She knew what was good for children, and a full stomach was very dangerous to their health. She also knew what was good for herself, so she kept for her own use the money that she was given for the children's food. The board responsible for the orphans sometimes checked on the health of the children, but they always sent the beadle, a kind of local policeman, to announce their visit the day before. So whenever the board arrived, of course, the children were always neat and clean.

This was the way Oliver was brought up. Consequently, at the age of nine he was a pale, thin child and short for his age. But despite frequent beatings by Mrs Mann, his spirit was strong, which was probably the reason why he managed to reach the age of nine at all.

On Oliver's ninth birthday, Mr Bumble the beadle came to the house to see Mrs Mann. Through the front window Mrs Mann saw him at the gate, and turned quickly to the girl who worked with her.

'Quick! Take Oliver and those others upstairs to be washed!' she said. Then she ran out to unlock the gate. (It was always kept locked to prevent official visitors walking in unexpectedly.)

'I have business to talk about,' Mr Bumble told Mrs Mann as he entered the house. He was a big fat man, often bad-tempered, and was full of self-importance. He did not like to be kept waiting at a locked gate.

Mrs Mann took his hat and coat, placed a chair for him, and expressed great concern for his comfort. 'You've had a long walk, Mr Bumble,' she said, 'and you must be thirsty.' She took out a bottle from the cupboard.

'No, thank you, Mrs Mann. Not a drop.' He waved the bottle away.

'Just a *little* drop, Mr Bumble, with cold water,' said Mrs Mann persuasively.

Mr Bumble coughed. 'What is it?' he asked, looking at the bottle with interest.

'Gin. I keep it for the children's medicine drink.'

'You give the children gin, Mrs Mann?' asked Mr Bumble, watching as she mixed his drink.

'Only with medicine, sir. I don't like to see them suffer.'

'You're a good woman, Mrs Mann.' Mr Bumble drank half his glass immediately. 'I'll tell the board about you. Now – the reason why I'm here. Oliver Twist is nine years old today. We've never been able to discover anything about his parents.'

'Then how did he get his name?'

'*I* gave it to him,' said Mr Bumble proudly. 'We follow the alphabet. The last one was an S – Swubble. Then it was T, so this one is Twist. The next one will be Unwin. Anyway, Oliver Twist is now old enough to return to the workhouse. Bring him here, please.' While Mrs Mann went to get him, Mr Bumble finished the rest of his gin.

Oliver, his face and hands now almost clean, was led into the room.

'Will you come along with me, Oliver?' asked Mr Bumble in a loud voice.

Oliver was very glad to be free of Mrs Mann's violence, but he said nothing because she was angrily shaking her finger at him. However, as the gate closed behind Oliver, he burst into tears. He was leaving behind the other children, the only friends he had, and he realized at that moment how lonely he was in the world.

Mr Bumble walked on with long steps, with Oliver on his short little legs running beside him. The feeling of contentment produced by gin-and-water had now disappeared, and the beadle was in a bad mood once more.

Back at the workhouse, Oliver was taken to see the board. He stood in front of ten fat men who were sitting around a table.

'What's your name, boy?' asked a particularly fat man with a very round, red face.

Oliver was frightened at the sight of so many people, and started to cry.

'Why are you crying?'

The beadle hit him on the back, and so naturally Oliver cried even more.

'The boy is a fool,' one member of the board announced.

'You know you have no father or mother,' said the first man, 'and that you have been brought up with other orphans?'

'Yes, sir,' replied Oliver, crying bitterly.

'Why is the boy crying?' repeated the other man, puzzled.

'You have come here to be educated,' continued the fat man, 'so you will start working here tomorrow at six o'clock.'

Oliver was led away to a large room, where, on a rough hard bed, he cried himself to sleep.

The room in the workhouse where the boys were fed was a large stone hall, and at one end the master and two women served the food. This consisted of a bowl of thin soup three times a day, with a piece of bread on Sundays. The boys ate everything and were always hungry. The bowls never needed washing. The boys polished them with their spoons until they shone. After three months of this slow starvation, one of the boys told the others he was so hungry that one night he might eat the boy who slept next to him. He had a wild hungry eye, and the other boys believed him. After a long discussion, they decided that one of them should ask for more food after supper that evening, and Oliver was chosen.

The evening arrived; the soup was served, and the bowls were empty again in a few seconds. Oliver went up to the master, with his bowl in his hand. He felt very frightened, but also desperate with hunger.

'Please, sir, I want some more.'

The master was a fat, healthy man, but he turned very pale. He looked at the little boy in front of him with amazement. Nobody else spoke.

'What?' he asked at last, in a faint voice.

'Please, sir,' replied Oliver, 'I want some more.'

The master hit him with the serving spoon, then seized Oliver's arms and shouted for the beadle. The beadle came quickly, heard the dreadful news, and immediately ran to tell the board.

'He asked for *more*?' Mr Limbkins, the fattest board member, asked in horror. 'Bumble – is this really true?'

'That boy will be hanged!' said the man who earlier had called Oliver a fool. 'You see if I'm not right.'

Oliver was led away to be locked up, and a reward was offered to anybody who would take him away and use him for work.

'Please, sir, I want some more.'

2

Oliver's first job

Oliver stayed a prisoner alone in the dark room for a week. He cried bitterly all day, and when the long night came, he spread his little hands over his eyes to shut out the darkness, and tried to sleep. He was given freezing water to wash with, and was beaten daily by Mr Bumble in front of all the other boys in the hall, as a warning to them.

One day Mr Bumble met the local undertaker, Mr Sowerberry, outside the workhouse.

'Do you know anybody who wants to train a boy for work, Mr Sowerberry?' Mr Bumble pointed at the notice on the wall above him, which offered five pounds to anybody who would take Oliver Twist for work.

Mr Sowerberry rubbed his chin and thought for a while. 'I pay enough for the poor with my taxes,' he said, 'so why shouldn't I be able to make use of them in my work? Yes, I'll take the boy myself.'

And so the board agreed to send Oliver to work for the undertaker. The necessary papers were signed. Oliver's small possessions were put into a brown paper parcel, and he was led to Mr Sowerberry's house by Mr Bumble. As they walked along, tears began to run down Oliver's face.

'What is it this time?' asked Mr Bumble impatiently. 'Don't be so ungrateful. This gentleman is going to look after you.'

'It's just that I'm so lonely, sir!' said the child. 'Everybody hates me. Please don't be angry with me, sir!'

Even Mr Bumble felt a little pity. He coughed, told Oliver to dry his eyes and be a good boy, and walked on with him in silence.

The undertaker had just finished work for the day when Mr Bumble entered his shop.

'Here, I've brought the boy,' said the beadle.

Oliver bowed to the undertaker, who raised his candle to get a better view of the boy. 'Mrs Sowerberry,' he called, 'come and have a look.'

His wife, a short, thin woman with a disagreeable face, came out to see. 'He's very small,' she said immediately.

'He is,' agreed Mr Bumble, 'but he'll grow, Mrs Sowerberry.'

'Yes,' she said crossly, 'when he eats our food. Go on, get downstairs.' She pushed Oliver downstairs into a damp, dark kitchen, and called to the girl working down there. 'Here, Charlotte, give this boy some meat that the dog left – if he thinks it's good enough for him.'

Oliver tore the meat to pieces with his teeth as if he were a wild animal. Mrs Sowerberry watched him in silent horror, already thinking about her future food bills, then took him upstairs to the shop.

'You'll sleep here, among the coffins,' she said.

Oliver stared around the dark, airless shop at the coffins, some finished, some only half-made. He trembled at the thought of ghosts. His bed was a small hole in the floor, and looked very like a grave.

But it was not only the room that depressed Oliver. He felt very lonely, with no friends and no one to care for him. As he lay on the bed, he found himself wishing that it really was his grave.

The next morning he was woken up by someone kicking at the shop door.

'Open the door, will you?' shouted a voice through the keyhole.

'Yes, sir.'

'I suppose you're the new boy,' said the voice through the keyhole. 'How old are you?'

'Ten, sir.'

'Then I'll hit you when I get in,' said the voice.

Oliver was experienced enough to know that the promise was probably true. He opened the door with a shaking hand, then looked up and down the street. All he could see was a large boy wearing the uniform of one of the charity schools, where the children of the very poor used to go.

'Did you want a coffin?' asked Oliver, innocently.

The charity-boy looked at him fiercely. 'You'll be needing a coffin soon, Workhouse, if you make jokes like that! I'm Mister Noah Claypole, and you're working under me. Now, hurry up and open the curtains!' As he said this, he kicked Oliver and entered the shop. He was a big, clumsy boy of about fourteen, with a large head and very small eyes. Added to these attractions were a red nose and dirty yellow trousers.

The boys went down to breakfast, which the girl Charlotte had made for them. She gave an extra piece of meat to Noah, then told Oliver to hurry up as it was his job to look after the shop.

'Did you hear that, Workhouse?' shouted Noah.

'He heard, Noah,' said Charlotte. 'Leave him alone.'

'Why?' asked Noah. 'All his relations have already left him alone. His mother and father aren't going to interfere with him!' Charlotte and Noah both started laughing loudly. Oliver sat alone in the corner, eating old bits of bread.

Noah was a charity-boy, but not a workhouse orphan; he at least knew who his parents were. But for a long time all the local shop-boys had insulted him because he wore the uniform of a charity-boy. Now fortune had brought him a creature in an even lower

9

position in society than himself. Noah intended to repay to Oliver every insult he had ever received, and to make the new boy's life a misery.

After a few weeks, Mr Sowerberry decided that he liked Oliver's appearance enough to train him in the undertaking business. Oliver's permanent expression of sadness was very suitable, the undertaker thought, for collecting dead bodies from houses and accompanying the coffins to funerals.

One day Mr Bumble came to tell them about a woman who had died in an extremely poor part of the town, and Sowerberry and Oliver went to collect the body. They went down dirty narrow streets where the houses on either side were tall and large, but very old. Some of the houses were almost falling down, and had to be supported by huge blocks of wood. The area was so poor that even the dead rats in the street looked as though they had died of hunger.

They found the right house, and climbed the dark stairs to a miserable little room. Some children watched them from the shadows as they entered. Something lay beneath a blanket on the floor in one corner. A man and an old woman stood near the body. Oliver was afraid to look at them. With their thin faces and sharp teeth, they looked like the rats he had seen outside.

As Sowerberry began to measure the body for a coffin, the man knelt on the floor and cried out, 'She starved to death, I tell you! That's why she died!' He fell to the floor, and all the children behind him started to cry. Sowerberry and Oliver, their work done, left as fast as they could.

They returned the next day with the coffin and four men from the workhouse who were to carry it. The man and the old woman followed the coffin to the church, and waited silently by the grave for the priest to arrive. When at last he came, he hurried through the burial prayers, and as quickly as possible (it was only a job, after all) the coffin was put into the ground. At this point the husband, who had not moved once during his wife's burial – not even during the long wait for the priest – suddenly fainted to the ground and had to have cold water thrown over him.

'So how did you like it, Oliver?' asked Sowerberry later, as they walked home.

'Not very much, sir,' Oliver answered truthfully.

'You'll get used to it, my boy.'

Oliver wondered how long that would take, and remained silent all the way back to the shop, thinking about everything that he had seen and heard.

3

Oliver goes to London

Oliver was now officially an undertaker's assistant. It was a good, sickly time of year, and coffins were selling well. Oliver gained a lot of experience in a short time, and was interested to see how brave some people were after a death in the family. During funerals for some rich people, for example, he saw that the people who had cried the loudest in church usually recovered the fastest afterwards. He noticed how in other wealthy families the wife or the husband often seemed quite cheerful and calm despite the recent death – just as if nothing had happened. Oliver was very surprised to see all this, and greatly admired them for controlling their sadness so well.

He was treated badly by most of the people around him. Noah was jealous because Oliver went out to burials while he was left back in the shop, so he treated him even worse than before. Charlotte treated him badly because Noah did. And Mrs Sowerberry was his enemy because Mr Sowerberry was supposed to be his friend.

One day something happened which might seem unimportant, but which had a great effect on Oliver's future. Noah was in a particularly bad mood one dinner-time, and so he tried to make Oliver cry by hitting him, pulling his hair, and calling him horrible names. This was all unsuccessful, so he tried personal insults.

'Workhouse, how's your mother?' he asked.

'She's dead,' replied Oliver, his face going red with emotion.

Noah hoped that Oliver was going to cry, so he continued. 'What did she die of, Workhouse?'

'Of a broken heart, I was told.' And a tear rolled down Oliver's cheek.

'Why are you crying, Workhouse?'

Oliver remained silent, and Noah grew braver. 'You know, I feel very sorry for you, Workhouse, but the truth is your mother was a wicked woman.'

Oliver seemed suddenly to wake up. 'What did you say?'

'She was so bad it was lucky she died, or she would have ended up in prison, or hung.'

His face bright red with anger, Oliver jumped up, seized Noah's throat, and shook the older boy so violently that his teeth nearly fell out. Then he hit him with all his strength and knocked him to the ground.

'He'll murder me!' screamed Noah. 'Charlotte! Help! Oliver's gone mad —'

Charlotte and Mrs Sowerberry ran in and screamed in horror. They took hold of Oliver and began to beat him. Then Noah got up

Charlotte took hold of Oliver and began to beat him.

and started to kick him from behind. When they were all tired, they forced Oliver, who was still fighting and shouting, into the cellar and locked it.

Mrs Sowerberry sat down, breathing heavily. 'He's like a wild animal!' she said. 'We could all have been murdered in our beds!'

'I hope Mr Sowerberry doesn't take any more of these dreadful creatures from the workhouse,' said Charlotte. 'Poor Noah was nearly killed!' Mrs Sowerberry looked at Noah sympathetically.

Noah, who was twice Oliver's size, pretended to rub tears from his eyes.

'What shall we do?' cried Mrs Sowerberry. 'He'll kick that door down in ten minutes.' They could hear Oliver banging and kicking at the cellar door. 'Noah – run and get Mr Bumble.'

So Noah ran through the streets as quickly as he could to fetch the beadle. When he reached the workhouse, he waited for a minute to make sure his face was suitably tearful and frightened.

As soon as Mr Bumble came out, Noah cried, 'Mr Bumble! Mr Bumble! It's Oliver Twist, sir. He's become violent. He tried to murder me, sir! And Charlotte, and Mrs Sowerberry as well.'

Mr Bumble was shocked and angry. 'Did he? I'll come up there immediately and beat him with my stick.'

When he arrived at the shop, Oliver was still kicking wildly at the cellar door.

'Let me out!' he shouted from the cellar, when he heard Mr Bumble's voice. 'I'm not afraid of you!'

Mr Bumble stopped for a moment, amazed and even rather frightened by this change in Oliver. Then he said to Mrs Sowerberry, 'It's the meat that's caused this, you know.'

'What?'

'Meat, madam. You've fed him too well here. Back in the workhouse this would never have happened.'

'I knew I was too generous to him,' said Mrs Sowerberry, raising her eyes to the ceiling.

At that moment Mr Sowerberry returned and, hearing what had happened (according to the ladies), he beat Oliver so hard that even

Mr Bumble and Mrs Sowerberry were satisfied. Mr Sowerberry was not a cruel man, but he had no choice. He knew that if he didn't punish Oliver, his wife would never forgive him.

That night, alone in the room with the coffins, Oliver cried bitter, lonely tears. He did not sleep, and very early in the morning, before anyone was awake, he quietly unlocked the shop door and left the house. He ran up the street and through the town as far as the main road, where he saw a sign that told him it was just seventy miles from there to London. The name London gave the boy an idea. That huge place! Nobody, not even Mr Bumble, could ever find him there! He had heard old men in the workhouse say it was a good place for brave boys, and that there was always work there for those that wanted it. It would be the best place for him. He jumped to his feet and walked forward again.

But after only four miles he began to realize just how far he would have to walk. He stopped to think about it. He had a piece of bread, a rough shirt, two pairs of socks and a penny. But he could not see how these would help him get to London any faster, so he continued walking.

He walked twenty miles that day. The only thing he had to eat was his piece of bread and some water which he begged from houses near the road. He slept the first night in a field, feeling lonely, tired, cold and hungry. He was even hungrier the next morning when he woke up, and he had to buy some more bread with his penny. That day he walked only twelve miles. His legs were so weak that they shook beneath him.

The next day he tried to beg for money, but large signs in some villages warned him that anyone caught begging would be sent to prison. Travellers on the road refused to give him money; they said he was a lazy young dog and didn't deserve anything. Farmers threatened to send their dogs after him. When he waited outside pubs, the pub-owners chased him away because they thought he had come to steal something. Only two people were kind enough to feed him: an old woman and a gate-keeper on the road. If they had not given him some food, he surely would have died like his mother.

Early on the seventh morning of his journey, Oliver finally reached the little town of Barnet, just outside London. Exhausted, he sat down at the side of the road. His feet were bleeding and he was covered in dust. He was too tired even to beg. Then he noticed that a boy, who had passed him a few minutes before, had returned, and was now looking at him carefully from the opposite side of the road. After a long time the boy crossed the road and said to Oliver,

'Hello! What's the matter then?'

The boy was about Oliver's age, but was one of the strangest-looking people he had ever seen. He had a dirty, ordinary boy's face, but he behaved as if he were an adult. He was short for his age and had little, sharp, ugly eyes. His hat was stuck on top of his head but it looked as though it would blow off at any minute. He wore a man's coat which reached almost down to his feet, with sleeves so long that his hands were completely covered.

'I'm very tired and hungry,' answered Oliver, almost crying. 'I've been walking for a week.'

'A week! The magistrate's order, was it?'

'The magistrate? What's that?'

'A magistrate's a kind of judge,' explained the surprised young gentleman. He realized Oliver did not have much experience of the world. 'Never mind that. You want some food,' he went on. 'I haven't got much money but don't worry – I'll pay.'

The boy helped Oliver to his feet, and took him to a pub. Meat, bread, and beer were placed before Oliver, and his new friend urged him to satisfy his hunger. While Oliver was eating, the strange boy looked at him from time to time with great attention.

'Going to London?' he asked him finally.

'Yes.'

'Got anywhere to live?'

'No.'

'Money?'

'No.'

The strange boy whistled, and put his arms into his pockets as far as the big coat sleeves would allow him. 'I suppose you want to sleep somewhere tonight, don't you?'

'I do,' replied Oliver. 'I haven't slept under a roof since I started my journey.'

'Well, don't worry. I've got to be in London tonight, and I know a very nice old gentleman there who'll let you live in his place and not even ask you for money!'

Oliver was deeply grateful for this offer of shelter and talked for a long time with his new friend. His name was Jack Dawkins, but he was usually called 'The Artful Dodger'. 'Artful' because he was very clever at getting what he wanted; and 'Dodger' because he was very good at not getting caught when he did something wrong. When he heard this, Oliver felt rather doubtful about having such a friend. However, he wanted first to meet the kind old gentleman in London, who would help him. After that, he could decide whether to continue the friendship with the Artful Dodger.

4

Oliver in London

For some reason the Dodger did not want to enter London during daylight, so it was nearly eleven o'clock at night when they got near the centre. Oliver had never seen a dirtier or more miserable place. The streets in this district were narrow and muddy, and there were terrible smells everywhere. Children wandered around even at this time of night, in and out of the many shops, playing and screaming. The pubs were full of people fighting, and big, evil-looking men stood in doorways or at dark corners. Oliver almost wanted to run away, but just then the Dodger pushed open a door and pulled Oliver into a dark hall.

'Who's there?' a voice cried out.

'It's me,' said the Dodger. The faint light of a candle appeared in the hall.

'Who's the other one?'

'A new friend.'

They went up some dark and broken stairs. Oliver could hardly see where he was going, but the Dodger seemed to know the way, and helped Oliver up. They entered a room with walls that were black with age and dirt. In front of the fire was a table with a candle stuck into a bottle of beer, and an old man, with a horribly ugly face and red hair, stood next to the fire cooking. He was wearing a dirty old coat and seemed to divide his attention between his cooking and a number of silk handkerchieves, which were hanging near the fire. There were several rough beds in the room. Four or five boys, about the same age as the Artful Dodger, sat round the table, smoking and drinking like middle-aged men. They all looked up when the

'My friend Oliver Twist,' the Dodger said to Fagin.

Dodger and Oliver entered.

'This is him, Fagin,' the Dodger said to the old man. 'My friend Oliver Twist.'

Fagin smiled and shook Oliver's hand. Then all the young gentlemen came up to him and shook both his hands very hard, especially the hand which held his few possessions. One of the boys was particularly kind. He even put his hands in Oliver's pockets so that Oliver would not have to empty them himself when he went to bed. The boys would probably have been even more helpful, but Fagin hit them on their heads and shoulders until they left Oliver alone.

'We're very glad to see you, Oliver,' said Fagin. 'I see you're staring at the handkerchieves, my dear. Aren't there a lot? We've just taken them all out to wash them, that's all! Ha! Ha! Ha!'

This seemed to be a joke, as the old gentleman and all his young friends gave loud shouts of laughter. Then supper began. Oliver ate his share of the food and was then given a glass of gin-and-water. Fagin told him to drink it fast. Immediately afterwards, Oliver felt himself lifted onto one of the beds and he sank into a deep sleep.

When he woke, it was late morning. Fagin was the only other person in the room, and he was boiling coffee in a pan. When the coffee was done, he turned towards Oliver and looked closely at the boy. Oliver was only just awake and his eyes were half-closed, so he seemed to be still fast asleep. Fagin then locked the door and from a hidden hole in the floor, he took out a small box, which he placed carefully on the table. His eyes shone as he opened it and took out a gold watch covered in jewels.

'Aah!' he said to himself. 'What fine men they were! Loyal to the end. They never told the priest where the jewels were. Nor about old Fagin. Not even at the very end. And why should they? It was already too late. It wouldn't have stopped the rope going round their necks!'

Fagin took out at least six more watches, as well as rings and bracelets and many other valuable pieces of jewellery. He looked at them with pleasure, then replaced them. 'What a good thing hanging is!' he murmured. 'Dead men can never talk, or betray old friends!'

At that moment he looked up and saw Oliver watching him. He closed the lid of the box with a loud crash, and picked up a bread knife from the table. 'Why are you watching me? What have you seen? Tell me – quick!'

'I couldn't sleep any longer, sir,' said Oliver, terrified. 'I'm very sorry.'

'You weren't awake an hour ago?' Fagin asked fiercely, still holding the knife.

'I promise I wasn't, sir,' replied Oliver.

'Don't worry, my dear,' Fagin said, putting down the knife and becoming once again the kind old gentleman. He laughed. 'I only tried to frighten you, my dear. You're a brave boy, Oliver! And did you see any of the pretty things?'

'Yes, sir.'

'Ah,' said Fagin, turning rather pale. 'They – they're mine, Oliver. All I have, in my old age.'

Oliver wondered why the old man lived in such an old, dirty place, when he had so many watches, but then he thought that it must cost Fagin a lot of money to look after the Dodger and the other boys. So he said nothing, and got up and washed. When he turned towards Fagin, the box had disappeared.

Soon the Dodger entered with a cheerful young man named Charley Bates.

'Have you been at work this morning?' Fagin asked the Dodger.

'Hard at work,' answered the Dodger.

'Good boys, good boys!' said Fagin. 'What have you got?'

'A couple of pocket-books and some handkerchieves.'

'Good workers, aren't they, Oliver?' said the old man.

'Very good,' said Oliver. The others all started laughing, though Oliver saw nothing funny in his answer. Fagin inspected the handkerchieves and told the two boys that they were extremely well made and that he was very pleased with their work.

After breakfast they played a very strange game. The cheerful old man put a watch in his jacket pocket, with a guard-chain round his neck, and a notebook and a handkerchief in his trouser pocket. Then he went up and down the room holding a walking stick, just like the old gentlemen who walked in the streets. Sometimes he stopped at the fireplace, and sometimes at the door, pretending to stare with great interest into shop windows. He would then constantly look round, as if afraid of thieves, touching all his pockets in such a natural and funny way that Oliver laughed until the tears ran down his face. All the time, the two boys followed Fagin everywhere, and every time he turned round, they moved out of his sight so quickly that it was impossible to follow their movements.

Finally, the Dodger bumped into him accidentally from behind, and at that moment both boys took from him, very quickly, his watch, guard-chain, handkerchief, and notebook. If the old man felt a hand in any of his pockets he cried out, and then the game began again.

Later, the boys went out again to do some more work. When they had gone, Fagin turned to Oliver. 'Take my advice, my dear,' he said. 'Make them your models. Especially the Dodger. He'll be a great man himself, and will make you one too, if you copy him. Is my handkerchief hanging out of my pocket, my dear?'

'Yes, sir,' said Oliver.

'See if you can take it out, without my feeling it. Just as you saw them doing it when we were playing.'

Oliver held up the bottom of the pocket with one hand, as he had seen the Dodger hold it, and pulled the handkerchief lightly out of it with the other.

'Has it gone?' asked Fagin.

'Here it is, sir,' said Oliver, showing it in his hand.

'You're a clever boy, my dear,' said the old gentleman, putting his hand on Oliver's head. 'I've never seen a quicker boy. If you go on like this, you'll be the greatest man in London. Now come here and I'll show you how to take the marks out of handkerchieves.'

Oliver wondered what the connection was between playing at stealing from the old gentleman's pocket and becoming a great man. But he followed him quietly to the table and was soon deeply involved in his new study.

Oliver remained in Fagin's room for many days, picking the marks and names out of the handkerchieves and sometimes playing the same game as before. One evening two young ladies came to visit, and a very cheerful party followed. Oliver thought they were very nice, friendly girls.

The Dodger and Charley Bates went out to work every day, but sometimes came home with no handkerchieves, and Fagin would get very angry. Once he even knocked them both down the stairs and sent them to bed with no dinner because they had returned with nothing.

At last, the morning came when Oliver was allowed to go out to work with the two other boys. There had been no handkerchieves for him to work on for several days and there was not very much to eat for dinner. The three boys set out, but they walked so slowly that Oliver thought they were not going to work at all. Then suddenly the Dodger stopped and put his finger to his lips.

'What's the matter?' demanded Oliver.

'Be quiet!' replied the Dodger. 'Do you see that old man outside the bookshop? He's the one.'

Oliver looked from the Dodger to Charley Bates with great surprise and confusion, but he had been told not to ask questions. The two boys walked quickly and secretly across the road towards the old gentleman. Oliver followed behind them, watching in silent amazement.

The old gentleman looked quite rich; he wore gold glasses, white trousers, and had an expensive walking stick under his arm. He had picked up a book and was standing there, reading it with great concentration – just as if he were in his own armchair at home. Oliver, his eyes wide with horror and alarm, watched as the Dodger put his hand in the old gentleman's pocket, took out a handkerchief, and handed it to Charley Bates. Then the two of them ran round the corner as fast as they could.

Suddenly, the whole mystery of the handkerchieves, and the watches, and the jewels, and Fagin, became clear. Oliver stood for a moment in terror, the blood rushing through him until he felt he was on fire. Then, confused and frightened, he started to run. At the same time, the old gentleman, putting his hand to his pocket and realizing his handkerchief was missing, turned round. He saw Oliver running away, so he naturally thought Oliver was the thief. With loud cries of 'Stop thief!', he ran after Oliver with the book still in his hand.

The old gentleman was not the only one who started shouting. The Dodger and Charley Bates, not wanting to attract attention to themselves by running down the street, had stopped round the first corner. When they realized what was happening, they also shouted 'Stop thief!' and joined in the chase like good citizens.

The cry of 'Stop thief!' always causes great excitement. Everybody

*Oliver, his eyes wide with horror and alarm, watched as the Dodger
put his hand in the old gentleman's pocket.*

in the street stopped what they were doing and began to shout
themselves. Many joined in the chase with enthusiasm and soon
there was a big crowd running after Oliver.

Finally, they caught the exhausted boy. He fell down on the pavement and the crowd gathered round him.

'Is this the boy?' they asked the old gentleman.

'Yes,' he answered, leaning over Oliver. 'But I'm afraid he's hurt himself.'

'*I* did that,' said a huge young man proudly. 'And I hurt my hand doing it.' The old gentleman looked at him with an expression of dislike.

Oliver lay on the ground, covered with mud and dust and bleeding from the mouth, and looked wildly at all the faces surrounding him. At that moment a policeman arrived and took Oliver by the collar. 'Come on, get up,' he said roughly.

'It wasn't me, sir,' said Oliver, looking round. 'It was two other boys. They're here somewhere.'

'Oh no, they aren't,' replied the policeman. In fact, he was right, as the Dodger and Charley had quietly disappeared as soon as the crowd had caught Oliver. 'Come on, get up!'

'Don't hurt him,' said the old gentleman.

'I won't,' said the policeman, tearing Oliver's jacket half off his back as he lifted him up.

The three of them started walking, followed by the excited crowd.

5

Oliver's life changes

Oliver was taken to the nearest police station. The officer at the gate looked at the boy. 'Another young thief, eh?' He turned to the old gentleman, 'Are you the person who was robbed, sir?'

'Yes, I am,' replied the old gentleman, 'but I'm not sure that this boy actually took the handkerchief. I don't really want to take him to court.'

'Too late. He must go before the magistrate now.'

Oliver was locked in a small stone cell, which was disgustingly dirty and smelly. As the key turned in the lock, the old gentleman said to himself thoughtfully, 'There's something in that boy's face . . . He could be innocent. Where have I seen someone like him before?' After thinking about this for a few minutes, he said, 'No; it must be imagination.' He sighed unhappily, and began reading the book again.

Some time later, the officer touched his shoulder and told him that the court was ready. A magistrate was a judge who dealt with small crimes in local courts, and the magistrate for this district was well known. His name was Mr Fang and he was a disagreeable, bad-tempered man. Today he was in a particularly bad mood. He frowned angrily at the old gentleman, and asked sharply,

'Who are you?'

'My name, sir, is Brownlow.'

'Officer! What is this man charged with?'

'He's not charged, sir,' answered the officer. 'He's accusing the boy.'

The magistrate looked at Mr Brownlow from head to foot. 'And what have you got to say?'

Mr Brownlow began to explain. 'I was standing outside a bookshop —'

'Be quiet, sir!' shouted Mr Fang. 'Policeman! Now – you arrested the boy. What happened?'

The policeman told the magistrate what he had heard, and how he had searched Oliver afterwards and found nothing.

'Are there any witnesses?' asked the magistrate.

'None,' answered the policeman.

Mr Fang then turned to Mr Brownlow and angrily told him to describe what had happened. Mr Brownlow explained that he had run after the boy only because he saw him running away. He did not think that the boy was the actual thief and he hoped that the boy would not be punished. 'He's been hurt already,' he added, 'and now I'm afraid he's very ill.'

'I don't believe that for a moment,' said Mr Fang unpleasantly. He turned to Oliver. 'Come now, don't try any clever tricks with me! What's your name?' he demanded.

Oliver tried to reply, but he was too weak to speak. He was deadly pale, and he felt the room spinning round him. At last he managed to whisper a request for water, but the magistrate refused angrily. Suddenly, Oliver fainted and fell to the floor.

Mr Fang stared at him angrily. 'Guilty. Three months' prison,' he said immediately. 'Let him lie there. He'll soon be tired of that.' Mr Fang stood up. 'This court is now closed.'

At that moment a man in an old black coat rushed in. 'Stop!' he shouted. 'Don't take the boy away. I saw it all. I'm the bookshop owner.'

Mr Fang's face was black with anger at this unexpected interruption, but the bookshop owner demanded to be heard. He described exactly what had really happened. He had seen two boys steal the handkerchief and then run away, leaving Oliver to be arrested.

In a final burst of bad temper, Mr Fang said that his time had been wasted. He announced that Oliver was innocent, and ordered everybody out of the court.

The order was obeyed, and as Mr Brownlow turned to go down

the street, he saw Oliver lying on the pavement, shaking, his face as white as death.

'Poor boy! Poor boy!' said Mr Brownlow, bending over him. He called a coach quickly, laid Oliver on the seat, and drove away.

The coach stopped at a neat house in a quiet, shady street in north London. Oliver was gently carried in to a bed, and received more care and kindness than he had ever had in his life. But he had a fever, and for many days he lay there unconscious. When he eventually awoke, weak, thin and pale, he looked anxiously around the room.

'What room is this? Where am I?' he said. 'This is not the place I fell asleep in.'

Mrs Bedwin, the motherly old housekeeper, heard his words, and instantly came to him. 'Hush – be quiet, my dear, or you'll be ill again. Lie down.'

He lay down, and woke up again much later. After a while, he was able to sit up in a chair, although he was still too weak to walk. In this new position he could see a picture of a woman hanging on the wall opposite. 'Who is that, madam?' he asked the old housekeeper.

'I don't know, my dear. Do you like it?'

'The eyes look so sad, and they seem to be staring at me. As if the person was alive, and wanted to speak to me but couldn't.'

'You're weak and nervous after your illness,' Mrs Bedwin said kindly. 'Don't worry about things like that.'

Later that day Mr Brownlow came in, having heard that the boy was a little better at last. He was delighted to see that Oliver could sit up. But when he saw Oliver's face clearly, Mr Brownlow stared hard at him.

'I hope you're not angry with me, sir,' said Oliver anxiously.

'No, no. Not in the least,' he replied. Then he turned to the housekeeper. 'But look, Mrs Bedwin, look there!' He pointed to the picture of the woman above Oliver's head and then to the boy's face. It was a living copy of the picture; even the expression was the same. Oliver did not understand what was happening. He was so alarmed by Mr Brownlow's excitement that he fainted once more.

The Dodger and Charley Bates had left the crowd which was chasing Oliver as soon as they could. They went back to their house through the narrow streets, using a complicated route in case anyone was following them. Once they were safely away from other people, Charley Bates rolled on the ground and laughed and laughed.

'Ha! Ha! Ha! When I saw Oliver running away so fast, round all the corners, bumping into walls . . . and all the time I had the handkerchief in my pocket . . . Ha! Ha! Ha!'

'But what'll Fagin say?' asked the Dodger.

'What do you mean?'

The Dodger said nothing more but led Charley Bates into the house and up the stairs. When Fagin saw them enter, he rose to his feet.

'Where's Oliver?' he asked them furiously.

The two boys looked uneasily at each other, but said nothing. Fagin took hold of the Dodger's collar and shook him violently. 'Tell me or I'll kill you!'

The Dodger slid out of his coat in one smooth movement, leaving Fagin holding only the empty coat. 'The police have got him,' he said reluctantly. He looked round for a weapon to fight with, but Fagin already had a heavy metal pot in his hand. He threw it hard at the Dodger, but missed and hit Charley Bates, who started to shout with fear.

Suddenly, all this noise and confusion was silenced by a deep voice at the door.

'What the devil's going on here?' the voice demanded.

The owner of the voice was a big man of about thirty-five in a black coat and very dirty trousers, with a brown hat on his head and a dirty handkerchief around his neck. He also had a three-day-old beard. A white dog with torn ears followed him into the room. The man kicked the dog into a corner and looked round at the signs of battle.

'Are they trying to murder you, Fagin? I would if I was them. I'd have done it long ago. Now, give me some beer, and don't poison it.'

It was said as a joke, but if the man had seen the evil look on Fagin's face, he might have thought the warning was a necessary one.

Fagin produced some beer, and as the fight appeared to be over, everybody sat down. In the conversation that followed, Fagin told the newcomer that Oliver had been caught by the police. 'I'm afraid, Mr Sikes,' he said, 'the boy may say something which will get us into trouble.'

'Very likely,' said Bill Sikes, smiling unkindly. 'You've got problems, Fagin.'

'And I'm afraid,' added Fagin, ignoring Sikes' remark, 'that if we're in trouble, then a lot of other people will be in trouble too, if you understand me, my dear.'

Sikes turned angrily towards the old man. There was a silence. Then Sikes said, 'Somebody must find out what's happened. If he hasn't said anything yet, we must catch him when he leaves the police station.'

Fagin nodded. But there was a difficulty. None of them wanted to go anywhere near a police station. The problem was solved with the arrival of the two young ladies whom Oliver had met one evening in Fagin's house.

'Nancy, my dear,' Fagin said. He smiled sweetly at one of the young ladies. 'Can you go to find out what's happened to Oliver?'

The young lady answered calmly, 'No, I won't.'

'You're the only one here that the police in this district don't know,' said Sikes. 'She'll go, Fagin.'

'No,' repeated Nancy.

'Yes, she will, Fagin.' Sikes was right. With a mixture of threats and promises, he soon persuaded Nancy to go.

She set off at once, and at the police station pretended to be a shy, frightened girl. 'Is my poor little brother Oliver here?' she asked the officer with the keys.

'He's not here,' the officer replied. 'The gentleman's got him.'

'The gentleman? Oh no! What gentleman?' cried Nancy, very upset.

The policeman explained that Oliver had become ill, and the old gentleman had taken him to his house in the Pentonville district of north London. Nancy, still looking terribly upset, left the station, and hurried back to Fagin's house with this news. As soon as he heard it, Sikes called his white dog, put on his hat and left without saying goodbye to anyone.

'We must find him,' Fagin said urgently to the rest of them. 'No one can stay here – it's too dangerous now. All of you – walk around Pentonville and keep your ears open. Don't come back until you have some news of Oliver! If you can, kidnap him! We've got to keep him quiet before he starts talking about us to his new friends.'

With these words, he pushed them all from his room and double-locked the door behind them. Then he took out his hidden box and very carefully hid all the watches and the jewellery beneath his clothes.

6

Oliver is found again

Oliver began to recover and slowly regain his strength. The picture that had caused Mr Brownlow's excitement was taken down from the wall, and was not mentioned again. Oliver was disappointed at the disappearance of the picture, since he liked the woman's face, but he had many other things to think about now.

They were happy days, while Oliver was getting better. He played cards with Mrs Bedwin and listened to stories about her family. The days were all so quiet and relaxing, after the hardships and poverty of his previous life. Mr Brownlow bought him a new suit and new shoes, and Oliver's dirty old clothes were given away.

One day Mr Brownlow asked him to come to his study for a little talk.

Oliver went in and sat down. He looked at Mr Brownlow's serious face in alarm. 'Don't tell me you're going to send me away, sir, please!' he exclaimed. 'Let me stay here! I could help with the housework . . . please, sir!'

'My dear child, don't be afraid,' said Mr Brownlow kindly. 'I won't desert you. I believe that you're a good boy, not a common thief. You told me you're an orphan – that seems to be the truth. But I want to hear now the whole story of your life, and how you came to be with the boys I saw you with that day.'

Oliver began his story but was soon interrupted by the arrival of Mr Grimwig, an old friend of Mr Brownlow's. Mr Grimwig was a fierce old gentleman and very fond of arguments. He clearly knew all about Oliver and inspected him closely.

'So this is the boy, is it?' he said at last.

Oliver bowed politely and was introduced by Mr Brownlow. Tea was then brought in, and during the meal Mr Grimwig stared so hard at Oliver that the boy felt rather confused. Eventually, Mr Grimwig whispered to Mr Brownlow, 'He may be a good-looking boy, but I think he's deceiving you, my good friend.'

'Nonsense!' said Mr Brownlow, becoming angry.

'Well, we'll see,' answered his friend. 'We'll see.'

Later that afternoon Mr Brownlow wanted to return some books to a bookseller, and to send some money for new books that he had already collected. Mr Grimwig suggested that Oliver should go. 'He'll be sure to deliver everything safely,' he said with a smile.

'Yes, please let me take them,' said Oliver, delighted to be of use.

Mr Brownlow hesitated, but Mr Grimwig's smile had annoyed him. 'Very well,' he said. 'Here are the books, Oliver, and a five-pound note. The bookseller will give you ten shillings change.'

'I won't be ten minutes,' replied Oliver eagerly, and he ran out into the street.

'So you expect him to come back, do you?' enquired Mr Grimwig.

'Yes, I do,' said Mr Brownlow, smiling confidently. 'Don't you?'

'No. He has a new suit of clothes, some valuable books, and a five-pound note in his pocket. He'll join his old friends the thieves, and laugh at you. If he comes back, I'll eat my hat.'

The two men sat by the window with a pocket-watch between them, and waited for Oliver's return.

Oliver hurried through the streets to the bookshop, thinking how lucky he was. Suddenly there was a loud scream behind him. 'Oh, my dear brother!' Before he could look round, a pair of arms was thrown tightly around his neck.

'Don't!' he cried, struggling. 'Let go! Why are you stopping me? Who is it?'

The young woman holding him started to cry loudly. 'I've found him! Oh! Oliver! You naughty boy, to make me suffer so much! Come home immediately, you cruel boy!' She burst into tears and several people stopped to stare at what was happening.

'What's the matter?' asked one of the watching women.

'He ran away from his parents a month ago,' the young woman said. 'They're hard-working, respectable people, and he left them to join a gang of thieves and bad characters, and almost broke his mother's heart.'

'Go home, you horrible child,' said another woman.

'Yes – go back to your parents,' said a third.

'But I haven't got any!' replied Oliver, greatly alarmed.'I haven't got a sister, either. I'm an orphan. I live in Pentonville.'

'Listen to him! Make him come home,' the young woman said to the crowd, 'or he'll kill his dear mother and father, and break my heart.'

Suddenly Oliver recognized the woman he had seen in Fagin's house. 'It's Nancy!' he said, without thinking.

'You see?' cried Nancy to the crowd. 'He knows me!'

Just then a big man ran out of a beer shop, followed by a white dog. 'What's this? Young Oliver! Come home to your poor mother, you young devil! And what books are these? You've stolen them, haven't you? Give them to me.' The man, who was Bill Sikes, seized Oliver with one strong hand and hit him on the head with the other.

'That'll do him good!' shouted some of the crowd. 'It's the only way to treat boys like him.'

Bill Sikes held onto Oliver's arm. 'Come on, you young thief!'

Still weak from illness, and terrified by the growling dog, Oliver

Bill Sikes held onto Oliver's arm. 'Come on, you young thief!'

could not resist. He was taken through the dark narrow streets at great speed. Sikes and Nancy gave him no chance to escape and Oliver had no breath to call out for help. All too quickly, he was back in Fagin's house, where his old friends were waiting for him.

'Delighted to see you looking so well, my dear,' Fagin said, bowing politely. 'Why didn't you write, and say you were coming? We'd have got something warm for supper.'

The Dodger and Charley Bates roared with laughter, and the

Dodger began looking through the books Oliver had with him.

'Give them back!' Oliver cried. 'Those books belong to the kind old gentleman who took me into his home. Send him back the books and the money – he'll think I stole them!'

'You're right,' laughed Fagin. 'He *will* think that!'

Oliver jumped to his feet and ran wildly from the room, shouting for help. The Dodger and Fagin caught him easily, and brought him back. Then the old man picked up a long piece of wood.

'So you wanted to get away, my dear, did you? Wanted to call the police and get help? We'll cure you of that.'

He hit Oliver hard on the shoulders with the stick. He was raising it for a second hit when Nancy rushed forward and, seizing the piece of wood, threw it into the fire.

'I won't let you do it, Fagin!' she shouted. 'You've got him again. Isn't that enough? Now leave him alone.'

Fagin and Sikes looked at each other, shocked by her reaction.

'You'd better keep quiet, my girl,' growled Sikes.

'No, I won't!' cried the girl wildly. 'Now you've got the boy, you'll turn him into a thief and a liar. Isn't that enough, without killing him too?'

She rushed at Fagin and would have hit him if Sikes had not held her arms so tightly that she couldn't move. She struggled wildly for a while, then, exhausted, she fainted. Sikes laid her down in the corner, as surprised as Fagin at her anger.

'She can be really wild when she's angry,' Sikes said.

Fagin wiped his forehead. 'That's the trouble with women,' he said, 'but she's a clever girl in her work.'

Then Charley Bates and the Dodger took away Oliver's expensive new suit, gave him some old clothes, and locked him up in a dark room. Oliver felt tired and ill, and was soon fast asleep.

7

The robbery

A few days later, a visitor arrived in London from Oliver's home town. He was a large, fat man, and very proud of his hat, which showed the world that he was a most important official. It was, in fact, Mr Bumble the beadle, Oliver's old enemy.

Mr Bumble had completed his business in the city, and had just finished a most satisfactory meal in a pub. He pulled up his chair to the fire, to enjoy his hot gin-and-water in comfort, and opened the newspaper. The first thing he saw was this notice:

A reward of five pounds is offered for any information leading to the discovery of a young boy, Oliver Twist, who was kidnapped from his home in Pentonville last Thursday evening. I am also very interested in any information about his past.

There was then a full description of Oliver's clothes and appearance, and Mr Brownlow's full address. Mr Bumble rubbed his eyes, read the notice again, and was at the address in less than ten minutes. He was shown into Mr Brownlow's study, where the old gentleman and his friend Mr Grimwig were sitting.

'Do you know where the poor boy is now?' Mr Brownlow asked, when the beadle had explained the reason for his visit.

Mr Bumble shook his head.

'Do you know anything *good* about him?' asked Mr Grimwig, looking closely at Mr Bumble's face.

Mr Bumble shook his head again, very seriously, and turned down the corners of his mouth.

'Then tell us everything you know about him,' said Mr Brownlow impatiently.

Mr Bumble put down his hat, unbuttoned his coat, folded his arms, and sat back in his chair. He spoke in his most important and official voice, and talked for twenty minutes. His listeners heard all the details of Oliver's illegitimate birth, and how generously he had been treated as a workhouse orphan. They heard how he had always been an ungrateful and dangerous child, violently attacking another boy, and finally running away from the house where he had been working.

The old gentleman shook his head sadly and gave Mr Bumble the five pounds. 'I would have been happy to give you three times the amount – if your story had proved that the boy was good.'

If Mr Bumble had known this earlier, he might have told a different story, but now it was too late. So he took the money and left.

Mr Brownlow walked up and down his room for several minutes, deep in thought. He rang the bell for Mrs Bedwin, his housekeeper, and told her what he had heard.

'I don't believe it,' she said, with great certainty.

'I was right,' said Mr Grimwig with satisfaction. 'You should have listened to what I said.'

Mr Brownlow said angrily, 'Never let me hear the boy's name again. Never. Remember that, Mrs Bedwin.'

There were sad hearts at Mr Brownlow's house that night.

* * *

Meanwhile, in another part of London, Oliver remained a prisoner. Fagin had told Oliver how ungrateful he had been to run away. He had told him that he would have died of hunger without Fagin's kindness. He went on to tell Oliver the story of another young boy, who had gone to the police to tell them about the gang, but who had finally been hanged one morning for being a thief. Fagin described the hanging in terrifying detail, and said that he hoped he would never have to tell the police about Oliver – and see Oliver with a rope around his neck. Oliver felt his blood turn cold.

He remained locked in a room for many days, seeing nobody between early morning and midnight. He spent his time thinking sadly about his friends in Pentonville. After a week he was free to wander round the house during the day. It was a dirty place, full of rats and insects but no other living thing. All the windows were closed, and covered with wood and metal bars that kept out the light.

One afternoon the Dodger and Charley Bates were at home and they started telling Oliver about their lives as thieves.

'Why don't you become one?' Charley asked him. 'We all are here – both of us, and Fagin, Sikes, Nancy . . . all of us.'

'I don't want to be,' replied Oliver. 'I wish they'd let me go.'

'But it's a good life,' the Dodger said, taking some coins from his pocket and throwing them up in the air. 'What does it matter where the money comes from?' he said, laughing. 'If you don't steal it, someone else will. You can be sure of that!'

Fagin entered at this point, with two young men, and joined in the conversation. One of the young men had just come out of prison, and there were many cheerful jokes about his very short hair-cut. Everybody sat around the fire, talking and laughing for hours. Fagin told Oliver how good the Dodger was at his job, and what a friendly boy Charley was. It was, without doubt, an interesting evening for Oliver, after so many days locked up alone.

After that evening he was rarely on his own again. He spent a lot of time with the Dodger and Charley, and often played the handkerchief game with them. At other times Fagin would tell them all about robberies he had committed in his younger days, telling the stories so well and putting in so many funny details that Oliver could not stop laughing, even though he knew it was wrong.

Fagin knew what he was doing. He had made sure that Oliver was so lonely and miserable that he would be desperate for any friends, however criminal. Slowly and deliberately, Fagin was trying to poison the young boy's mind.

One damp, cold, windy night a few weeks later, Fagin put on his heavy coat and, with the collar pulled up high to hide his face, left his home. He walked fast through the streets, never losing his way even in the darkest places. Finally, he reached an evil, narrow street lit only by a single lamp. He knocked on a door, said something quietly to the person who opened it, then walked upstairs.

Bill Sikes was sitting by his fire with his dog when Fagin entered. The room was a small, dark place with almost no furniture. Nancy was there, too, and Fagin glanced at her uneasily. He had not seen her since she had attacked him to stop him hitting Oliver. However, she seemed to have forgotten all about it, because she told him to pull up a chair and warm himself by the fire.

'I'm ready for business,' Bill Sikes said, looking at Fagin suspiciously. 'Say what you have to say, Fagin.'

'It's about the robbery at Chertsey, Bill,' answered Fagin. 'Some lovely silver in that house down there!'

'I know, I know,' Sikes said. 'I was down there two nights ago to have a look at the house. But it's locked like a prison at night, all except one part.'

'Where's that?' asked Fagin, bending his head forwards, his eyes staring excitedly at Sikes.

'Do you think I'm stupid? I'm not telling you! Anyway, what we need is a boy.'

'So there's a small place where only a boy can enter the house?' asked Fagin.

'Maybe. But we need a boy.'

There was silence for a time, while Fagin thought. Then he made a sign to Sikes to tell Nancy to leave the room.

'Don't worry,' Sikes said. 'You can trust her – *she* won't talk. Isn't that right?'

'Of course it's right,' answered the young woman, taking a large drink from the bottle on the table, and laughing. 'Anyway, Fagin, I know your idea is for Oliver to do the job.'

'You're a clever girl,' said Fagin, smiling evilly. 'That's exactly what I had in mind. Listen, Bill – the boy's been training for a few weeks, and it's time he did some work. He's the smallest one, anyway.'

'Is he safe?' asked Sikes. 'Because if he tries any tricks on me, I'll kill him!'

'He'll be ours for life, if he feels he's one of us. And this job will make him feel like that,' said Fagin eagerly. 'The boy looks so innocent he's perfect. And we've got to include him in some crime as soon as we can. Otherwise, if he escapes now, he can tell the police about us and stay free himself.'

So it was decided that Oliver would help Sikes with the robbery in two days' time. The plan was discussed in great detail and all the arrangements made. By then, Sikes was very drunk, and Fagin got up to leave. As he put on his coat, he stared hard at Nancy, frowning a little. No, he was sure he could trust her; she was loyal.

The next night, Oliver was alone in Fagin's house when Nancy entered. She was so nervous and white-faced that Oliver asked her if she was ill.

'God forgive me!' she said, beating her hands together. 'I never thought I would do this!'

'Has anything happened?' asked the boy. 'What is it?'

She sat with her back to him, and hid her face with her hands. After a while she said, 'I don't know why I feel so strange sometimes. Come on, Oliver – are you ready? You have to come with me to Bill's house.'

'Why?'

'Oh – nothing important.'

Oliver did not believe her, but he thought that at last this might be an opportunity to escape. So he said, rather too quickly, 'I'm ready.' Nancy guessed what he was thinking.

'Oliver,' she said, 'this is not the time to escape. I've saved you once, and I will again, but if anything happens tonight, it might mean my death.' She said this so seriously that Oliver decided it must be true. He was quiet while they walked quickly through the streets to Sikes' house.

Inside his room, Sikes sat Oliver down on a chair. 'Did he come quietly?' he asked Nancy.

'Quiet as a mouse.'

'Glad to hear it,' said Sikes. 'Now listen to me, boy.' He put a gun against Oliver's head. 'If you say one word when you're outside with me, I'll shoot you. Understand?'

Oliver nodded, trying hard not to tremble.

Sikes and Oliver started out at five o'clock in the morning, while it was still dark. They crossed from one side of London to the other. At first the streets were empty, then shops began to open and people started going to work. Gradually, the noise and traffic increased, and as they passed through the meat market at Smithfield, Oliver was amazed by the sight and smells of so many animals, and by the huge crowds of people, all pushing and swearing and shouting. But Bill Sikes marched on without stopping.

Later in the day they were given a lift in a horse and cart from west London out into the country. Night fell, and after walking a few more miles down country roads, they finally arrived at an old house standing alone by a river. It was dark and seemed to be empty. They went inside without knocking.

Inside were two other men, who, at Sikes' command, produced food and drink for him and the boy. Then Sikes told Oliver to get some sleep as they would be going out again later that night. Oliver still had no idea of the purpose of this expedition, but his head ached with tiredness and he soon fell asleep.

At half past one the men got up and checked their equipment, gathering several sticks as well. Sikes and the man called Toby left the house together, with Oliver walking between them. There was now a thick fog and the night was very still as they hurried through the deserted streets of the nearby town. Out in the country again, they walked down several small roads until finally they stopped at a house surrounded by a high wall. As quick as lightning, Toby climbed up and pulled Oliver after him. Inside the garden, they crept towards the house, and now, for the first time, Oliver realized in horror that the purpose of the expedition was robbery, and maybe even murder.

Bill Sikes broke open a small window at the back of the house, then shone his light into Oliver's face.

'Now listen. I'm going to put you through here. Go straight through into the hall and on to the front door, and let us in. And if you don't, you can be sure I'll shoot you.'

Oliver, stupid with terror, was lifted through the window into the house. Desperately, he decided to try to run upstairs and warn the family. He began to creep forwards.

Suddenly, there was a loud noise from the hall.

'Come back!' shouted Sikes. 'Back! Back!'

Oliver stood still, frozen with fear. A light appeared, then two men on the stairs, then a sudden bright flash, and a loud bang. Oliver staggered back. Sikes seized the boy's collar through the window and pulled him back out into the garden.

'They've hit him!' shouted Sikes. 'He's bleeding.'

A bell rang loudly, above the noise of more gunshots and the shouts of men. Oliver felt himself being carried across rough ground, and then he saw and heard no more.

8

After the robbery

The night was bitterly cold. A sharp wind whipped the fallen snow up into the air and blew it into every hole and corner. It was a night for the homeless to lie down and die; and for luckier people to sit close to their fires and thank God they were at home.

In the workhouse where Oliver was born, Mrs Corney – the widow in charge – was making tea by her fire. When she heard a knock at her door, she frowned and called out sharply, 'Come in.' The frown, however, was quickly changed to a sweet smile when

45

There was a sudden bright flash and a loud bang.
Oliver staggered back.

she saw Mr Bumble enter.

'Hard weather, Mr Bumble,' said the widow.

'Yes, indeed, ma'am,' replied the beadle. 'We've had to give out to the poor people in this town great quantities of bread and cheese today, and they're still complaining. Why, one man even came back and demanded some free fire-wood! What does he want that for? People are never satisfied. Give them one thing today, and tomorrow they'll ask for something else!'

Mrs Corney agreed that it was very shocking. They discussed some workhouse business together, and then Mr Bumble looked hopefully at the teapot. Mrs Corney offered him some tea. Instantly, Mr Bumble sat down by the fire and gave the widow such a warm smile that her face turned a delicate pink. She passed Mr Bumble the tea-cup, and as he took it, he managed to give her hand a little stroke. 'You're a kind-hearted woman, Mrs Corney,' said the beadle.

'Oh, Mr Bumble!' said the widow, smiling shyly. For a while there was a friendly silence between them, then Mr Bumble moved his chair closer to the widow's. Mrs Corney, of course, did not notice this, but when the beadle's arm began to slide around her waist, she felt she must make a small protest.

Encouraged by this response, Mr Bumble immediately gave her a kiss, but at this interesting moment there was a sudden knock at the door. Mr Bumble jumped to his feet and went to the other end of the room.

'Please, Mrs Corney,' said a voice outside. 'Old Sally is going fast.'

'Well, what can I do to help her?' asked Mrs Corney angrily.

'Nothing, ma'am,' replied the old woman outside. 'But she says she has something to tell you, which you must hear. She won't die quietly till you come.'

Complaining loudly, Mrs Corney asked Mr Bumble to wait until she came back. Then she followed the old woman up the stairs.

Old Sally lay in bed in a freezing cold room. The fire was so small and mean that it gave no warmth at all.

Mrs Corney bent over the bed, and the dying woman opened her eyes. 'Come closer,' she murmured. 'Let me whisper in your ear.' She held onto Mrs Corney's arm and pulled her down towards her. 'In this same room I once helped a pretty young woman who came in with cut and bleeding feet, who gave birth to a boy and then died.'

'Well?' asked Mrs Corney impatiently.

'I robbed her. She was hardly dead before I stole it!'

'Stole what?'

'*It!* The only thing she had. It was gold. It could have saved her life!'

'Gold? Who was this mother? Tell me!'

'She told me to look after it when she died.' The old woman's mind was getting confused. 'She trusted me, poor girl, and I stole it.'

'Quick, tell me or it may be too late!' said Mrs Corney greedily. 'What was it, and what was the boy's name?'

The old woman could hardly speak. 'Oliver. The gold I stole was —'

'Yes, yes! What?'

The old woman fell back onto the bed, dead.

Mrs Corney hurried back to her room, where Mr Bumble was still admiring her furniture and counting her silver tea-spoons. They sat down again by the fire, and soon Mr Bumble's arm returned to its previous position round Mrs Corney's waist. It was not long before he asked her to marry him, and the widow happily accepted him. While they drank to celebrate the arrangement, Mrs Corney told Mr Bumble about old Sally's death, and the unknown gold object which she had stolen from the dead body of the young woman.

After many expressions of undying love, Mr Bumble finally left the room and returned home, with bright visions of his future.

While these events were happening in the workhouse, the Artful Dodger and Charley Bates were playing cards in Fagin's house. The Dodger, as usual, was winning easily; somehow, he always seemed to know exactly what cards the other players had in their hands. Suddenly there was a faint ring on the bell downstairs, and Toby came in – the man who had gone with Bill Sikes and Oliver to rob the house in Chertsey. Fagin jumped to his feet.

'Where are they?' he screamed. 'Sikes and the boy! Where are they hiding?'

'We failed,' said the robber.

'What happened?'

'They fired and hit the boy. We ran away with Oliver between us, and they chased us with dogs.'

'And the boy? What about the boy?' gasped Fagin.

'His head was hanging down, and he was cold. We needed to go faster so we left him in a field, alive or dead. That's all I know about him.'

Fagin did not wait to hear any more. He gave an angry scream, ran out of the house and hurried through the streets until he reached Bill Sikes' house. As he climbed the stairs, he thought, 'Well, Nancy, if there's anything going on here, I'll find out about it – however clever you are.'

Nancy was alone upstairs in her room, her head on the table.

'She's been drinking again,' thought Fagin. As he closed the door, she woke up. He told her what had happened during the robbery; she said nothing and her head returned to the table. 'And where do you think the boy is now, my dear?' Fagin asked her, trying hard to see her face. 'Poor little child! Left alone like that.'

Nancy looked up. 'I hope the child's dead. Then he'd be happier than any of us.'

'What!' said Fagin, in amazement.

'It's better like that. The sight of the boy turns me against myself, and all of you.'

'You're drunk.' Fagin suddenly lost his temper. 'The boy's worth a fortune to me – and now a drunken gang has lost him. And if Sikes doesn't return that boy to me, dead or alive, I'll tell the police about him and I'll get Sikes hanged. Just remember that!'

When Fagin left her, Nancy was already back in a drunken sleep, her head lying on the table once more. Fagin went out into the blackness of the night and walked home. He had reached the corner of his street and was searching in his pocket for his key, when a dark figure came out of the shadows and crossed the road towards him.

'I've been waiting here for two hours, Fagin,' said the stranger. 'Where have you been?'

'On your business, my dear,' said Fagin, glancing at him uneasily.

'We'd better talk inside.'

The door closed behind them and they crept quietly up to the top floor in order not to wake the sleeping boys downstairs. They sat in a dark room, the only light coming from a candle burning in the passage outside.

The stranger's name was Monks, and he was in an evil mood.

He listened to Fagin for a while, frowning heavily. 'It was badly planned,' he said angrily. 'Couldn't you have made the boy into an ordinary thief, and then got him arrested and sent out of the country for the rest of his life?'

'But he isn't like the other boys here,' Fagin said. 'I had nothing to frighten him with. Anyway, I've already helped you. After he was caught by the police, stealing from the bookshop, I got Nancy to get him back. And then she felt sorry for him.'

'Kill her!' Monks said impatiently.

'We can't afford to do that kind of thing,' said Fagin. 'But I can turn the boy into an ordinary thief now. And then Nancy will harden her heart against him. I know how women are. But if he's already dead —'

'That's not my fault!' said Monks quickly. 'I always said to you – do anything you want to him, but don't kill him. I wouldn't have been able to forget it, if you had.'

Suddenly he jumped to his feet, staring at the wall opposite the door. 'What's that?' he whispered, terrified.

'What? Where?' cried Fagin.

'The shadow! I saw the shadow of a woman pass along that wall!'

White-faced, they both ran from the room into the passage. The candle threw long shadows down the stairs, but there was no one there. They listened. Only silence filled the house.

'It was your imagination,' said Fagin, softly.

'I swear I saw it!' replied Monks. They searched all the upstairs rooms. They were empty, and as quiet as death. Monks grew calmer, and eventually left the house at one o'clock in the morning.

The chase down at Chertsey the previous night had not lasted long. There was a lot of noise of men shouting and dogs barking, as the servants from the house pursued the robbers across the fields. But Sikes and Toby wasted no time. They dropped Oliver's unconscious body in a field, and disappeared into the fog and the darkness in different directions. The three pursuers lost enthusiasm for the chase and agreed among themselves that it was much too dangerous to continue. They returned to the house, keeping close together and trying to look brave.

Morning came, but Oliver still lay in the field as if dead. It began to rain heavily, and after a while Oliver opened his eyes. His left arm was covered in blood and hurting badly. He felt so weak he could hardly stand, but he knew that if he stayed where he was, he would die. Gasping with pain, he forced himself to his feet and with slow, shaky steps, began to walk. He had no idea where he was going, and moved forward mechanically, as though in a dream.

After a while his feet found a road, and he looked round and saw a house in the distance. He decided he would rather die near human beings than in a cold field, so he turned his steps towards the house. As he came nearer, he realized that the house was familiar and he felt faint with terror. But where else could he go? With a last effort, he crawled up the path and knocked on the door, then fell exhausted on the step.

It was now mid-morning. Inside the house the men servants were still describing the night's adventures to the cook and the servant girl, who gasped with appreciative horror at every exciting moment. They were all enjoying themselves very much – when there came a knock at the door. Pale with fright, they all stared at each other. Nobody was keen to answer the knock, so eventually they all went, including the dogs. Very cautiously, they opened the door, and saw nothing more alarming than poor Oliver, curled up in a sad little heap on the step.

Then one of the men gave a shout, seized the boy by a leg and pulled him into the hall. 'Here he is!' he cried excitedly. 'Here's the thief! I shot him last night!'

*They opened the door and saw poor Oliver, curled up
in a sad little heap on the step.*

A young lady appeared at the top of the stairs. 'What's going on
here? Quiet, please! Is this poor boy very hurt?'

'Very,' said the servant, proudly.

'Then one of you go to town as fast as you can and fetch a policeman and Dr Losberne. The rest of you, help to carry the boy upstairs and put him to bed. Treat him kindly, I beg you.'

9

Oliver starts another life

In a comfortable, pleasant sitting-room, the two ladies of the house waited anxiously for the doctor and the police to arrive. The owner of the house, Mrs Maylie, was an older woman, but her niece, Rose, was a girl of seventeen, whose quiet beauty and gentle charm won all hearts.

As soon as the doctor arrived, he ran breathlessly into the house and burst into the room without knocking. He was clearly a good friend of the ladies.

'I never heard of such a dreadful thing! You should both be dead of fright!' he said to Mrs Maylie. 'In the silence of the night, too! Are you both all right? Why didn't you send for me at once?'

'We are quite all right,' said Rose, smiling. 'But there's an injured boy upstairs whom aunt wants you to see.'

Dr Losberne went up to examine Oliver, and was there for some time. He came down looking rather puzzled, and asked the two ladies to see the boy with him.

'I can promise you there's nothing very frightening about him,' he said.

Instead of the evil-looking robber they expected to see, the two ladies found only a pale, thin child, lying peacefully asleep.

He looked so innocent that Mrs Maylie said, 'This child could never have been in a gang of robbers!'

'It certainly seems strange,' agreed the doctor, 'but wickedness can hide behind the most gentle face, you know.'

'But he's so young, too!' cried Rose. 'Can you really believe this poor boy is a criminal? Oh, Dr Losberne, and my dear aunt, I beg you both to have pity on him.'

Mrs Maylie did not need persuading, and the doctor could not resist Rose's tears. He had, in fact, an extremely kind heart, which he tried to hide behind a quick, fierce manner – though this usually deceived no one.

'Well, what's to be done, then?' he said quickly. 'We'll have the police here at any moment, ready to take the boy away and throw him into prison!'

Rose begged him to think of a plan, and the doctor thought hard for a few minutes, frowning fiercely. At last he said, 'I've got it!' and rubbed his hands together in satisfaction.

A little later, Oliver woke up and was very anxious to tell his story, although he had lost a lot of blood and was very weak. When the doctor and the ladies had heard all about his sad life, they were quite sure that they wanted to save Oliver from any unfair punishment. So Dr Losberne went down to the kitchen to talk to the three servants who had surprised Sikes and Oliver during the robbery. The doctor folded his arms and gave the men a long, hard stare.

'Tell me,' he began, 'can you be *absolutely sure* that the boy upstairs is the same one that was in the house last night? Well?'

The doctor, usually such a friendly man, seemed so angry that the servants stared at him, open-mouthed. The doctor gave them no time to think, and went on fiercely,

'Three men see a boy for about a second in the dark, in the

middle of a lot of smoke and noise. A boy comes to the same house the next day and because one arm is injured, they think he must be the robber. Are you going to swear that this is the same boy? Well? What do you say?' he finished impatiently.

The servants looked at each other in great confusion. Suddenly there was a ring at the gate; the police officers had finally arrived. Dr Losberne gave orders that plenty of beer should be served before the officers went up to see Oliver. He also made sure that the servants had a generous amount of beer, too.

When the officers were finally allowed to see Oliver, Dr Losberne said, 'This is a boy who was shot this morning while walking on a farmer's property where he shouldn't have been. The servants saw him and immediately thought he must be the same boy from last night. But now they say they're sure it's *not* the same boy.'

The servants were by now so confused by beer and excitement that they were not sure of anything at all. The robbers had certainly had a boy with them, they said, but whether this boy was the same boy . . . well, it seemed very doubtful. The police, too, had drunk quite a lot of beer by now, and before long they were very willing to believe that Oliver was not the robber of the night before. They had their own ideas about who committed all the robberies in the area, and Oliver was unknown to them.

At last the police left, and Oliver was allowed to recover in the kind care of Mrs Maylie, Rose, and Dr Losberne. It was several weeks before he was well enough to get out of bed. But then he quickly grew stronger, and every day told his rescuers how grateful he was. One thing, however, caused him unhappiness. He wanted to find Mr Brownlow, the kind old man who had looked after him in London. 'Mr Brownlow would be pleased to know how happy I am now,' he said. So when Dr Losberne offered to take Oliver to

London to see Mr Brownlow, the boy was very pleased.

They set out by coach one fine morning, and when they arrived in London, they went straight to Mr Brownlow's house. Oliver's heart beat with excitement as they stopped outside. But the house was empty. They were told by the people next door that Mr Brownlow had moved to the West Indies six weeks before. Oliver was very disappointed; he had thought about Mr Brownlow so much recently, and had always hoped to find him again. But now the kind old man had moved abroad, still believing Oliver was a lying thief, and he might hold this belief until the day he died.

This was a bitter disappointment to Oliver, but his new friends were still as kind to him as ever. They left the house in Chertsey and moved to a quiet cottage in the country, taking Oliver with them. Spring came, and in the fresh air, away from the noise and smoke and trouble of the city, Oliver began a new life. He went for walks with Rose and Mrs Maylie, or Rose read to him, and he worked hard at his lessons. He felt as if he had left behind forever the world of crime and hardship and poverty.

10

Life in the country

The weeks slipped contentedly past, and spring turned into summer. Oliver was now a strong and healthy boy, and very fond of Rose and Mrs Maylie – as they were of him.

One hot summer evening, after a walk in the country, Rose became very weak and pale, and confessed she felt ill. By the next morning she was in a dangerous fever, and Mrs Maylie and Oliver were afraid she might die. Mrs Maylie sent Oliver to the nearest town, four miles away, to post two express letters. One was to Dr Losberne in Chertsey, the other to Harry Maylie, Mrs Maylie's son.

Oliver, filled with anxiety, ran as fast as he could along the country roads and across the fields until, hot and exhausted, he reached the town. He posted the letters and turned to hurry home again. As he was running past a pub in the main street, he accidentally bumped into a tall man in black coming out. The man stared at Oliver. 'What the devil's this?' he said, stepping back.

'I'm sorry, sir. I was in a hurry, and didn't see you.'

The man murmured angrily to himself, 'Who would have thought it? Curse him! I can't get away from him!'

'I'm sorry, sir,' repeated Oliver, frightened by the man's wild, staring eyes.

'The devil break your bones!' the man said through his teeth. 'What are you doing here?' He raised his hand and started towards Oliver with a mad look in his eyes, but fell violently to the ground, shaking and gasping, in a fit. People hurried up and helped the man into the pub while Oliver, thinking that the man was mad, ran quickly home.

Mrs Maylie and Oliver passed a sleepless night, and Rose grew steadily worse as the fever burned in her. Oliver said every prayer he had ever learnt ten times over.

Late the next day Dr Losberne and Harry Maylie arrived, and the house was full of worried faces and anxious whispers. But the danger passed, and by the next night Dr Losberne was able to announce that, though seriously ill, Rose would not die. Oliver cried for joy.

A day or two later, Mrs Maylie talked privately to her son. Harry was a handsome young man of about twenty-five, with a cheerful, honest face and friendly manners. He was clearly very fond of Rose.

'I know that you want to marry Rose,' Mrs Maylie told her son, 'and she is the nicest person I know. But I want you to remember one thing – her birth.'

'Mother, that means nothing to me,' said the young man. 'I love her.'

'I know you do, Harry, but she herself is well aware of her doubtful birth, and this might affect her answer if you ask her to marry you. I know you have ambitions to enter politics. If you marry a woman with a stain on her name, even though it's not her fault, it might spoil your chances of success in life. Society is cruel, Harry. People might use the knowledge of your wife's doubtful birth against you, and against your children, too. And one day, you might begin to regret your marriage.'

'Only a selfish man would do that, Mother!' Harry answered impatiently. 'No, I am quite determined. I have loved Rose for a long time, and nothing will ever change that.'

Mrs Maylie sighed. 'And she, I know, is very fond of you. But she herself may try to protect you, and refuse an offer of marriage from you, for your sake. Remember that, Harry. But now, I must go back and sit with her.'

'Will you tell her how much I've worried about her?' asked Harry. 'And how anxious I am to see her again?'

'Of course I will,' replied Mrs Maylie.

Some days after this conversation, Oliver was sitting in the room where he studied in the evenings. It was a warm night, and he had been studying hard for some hours. He fell asleep at his desk and started dreaming. He dreamt that he was in Fagin's house again, and could see the old man sitting in his corner, whispering to another man. 'Yes, my dear,' he heard Fagin say, 'you're right.

*In his dream, Oliver heard Fagin say, 'Yes, my dear, you're right.
That's him.'*

That's him.'

In Oliver's dream the other man answered, 'Of course it is! I told you I'd seen him. I'd recognize him anywhere. If I walked across his unmarked grave, I'd know it was him buried under the ground.'

He said this with such hatred that Oliver woke up from fear. In front of him, at the open window, so near he could almost touch them, were Fagin and the strange, wild man he had bumped into outside the pub in the town. In a flash, they were gone. Oliver sat still, white with terror, for a second, then shouted loudly for help.

Harry and Dr Losberne came running, and hearing what had happened, they rushed outside into the night and searched the garden and the fields around. There was no sign of anybody.

'It must have been a bad dream, Oliver,' said Harry, breathless after running through the fields. He had heard all about Oliver's past from his mother.

'No,' replied Oliver, still frightened. 'I saw them both as plainly as I see you now.'

Nothing more was seen or heard of the two men, and after a few days, the event was forgotten. Rose recovered rapidly and was soon able to go outside again. Harry Maylie waited a few days, then, as his mother had expected, he asked Rose to marry him. And as his mother had warned him, Rose refused.

'Don't you love me?' he asked her, holding her hand.

'I do,' she whispered, 'but please try to forget me. It would ruin your future as a politician if anybody found out about my birth. I could never, never forgive myself.'

Harry paused for a few minutes. 'Tell me one thing, dear Rose. Could you have accepted if your past had been different? Or if I had been poor and friendless, with no hope of riches or success?'

'I could,' answered Rose, covering her face to hide her tears. 'But as you are, I can never be more than a friend to you.'

'I shall ask you once more,' said Harry softly. 'In a year's time or less, I shall ask you to change your mind.'

The girl shook her head and smiled sadly. 'No, it will be useless.'

Harry left the next day, having asked Oliver to write to him secretly with news of his mother and Rose. From an upstairs window, Rose watched him leave with tears in her eyes.

Mr Bumble was now a married man, and not a happy one. He was no longer a beadle but the manager of the workhouse, and his wife, formerly Mrs Corney, scolded and argued with him day and night. One evening, after a particularly violent fight, when she threw things at him and chased him out of the house, he went for a walk alone through the town. He felt very sorry for himself, and finally went into a pub to find comfort in gin-and-water. A tall dark man, sitting in the corner, watched Mr Bumble while he drank. The stranger's clothes were dusty and muddy, as if he had travelled a long way. Mr Bumble began to feel uncomfortable at the man's hard stare, and tried to avoid meeting his eyes.

'I've seen you before,' the stranger said, eventually. 'You were the beadle here.'

'I was. But I don't recognize you.'

'It doesn't matter. I came here to look for you, and I'm lucky to have found you. I'd like some information.' He pushed a couple of coins across the table.

'What information?' asked Mr Bumble suspiciously, slipping the coins into his pocket.

'About a workhouse birth. A boy called Oliver Twist.'

'Young Twist! I remember him! He was a dreadful —'

'It's not him I want to talk about,' interrupted the stranger. 'I've heard enough of him. It's the old woman who was the nurse for his mother. Where is she?'

'Oh – she died last winter,' said Mr Bumble. Then he remembered that his wife had been there when old Sally had died, and he realized that this information might be worth something. He told the man that one woman had been with the nurse when she died, and had heard some secret from her.

'Where can I find this woman?' the stranger asked quickly, showing in his pale face how important this was to him.

'I can bring her to meet you tomorrow,' said Mr Bumble.

'All right. Down by the river, at nine in the evening.' The man wrote the address on a piece of paper.

'And your name?' asked Mr Bumble.

'Monks,' replied the stranger, 'but you don't need to remember it.' Then he quickly left the pub.

The next evening was dark and cloudy; a storm threatened and already the first drops of rain were falling. Mr and Mrs Bumble walked up the main street of the town, then turned towards a group of ruined old houses next to the river. Mr Bumble went first, carrying a dim light, and his wife followed closely behind. At the oldest and most ruined building, they stopped and Mr Bumble took out his piece of paper. The first distant crash of thunder shook the air, and the rain began to pour down heavily. Then they heard Monks calling out of an upstairs window.

'Is that the man?' Mrs Bumble asked her husband.

'Yes.'

'Then be careful to say as little as you can. Don't tell him I'm your wife.'

Monks opened a small door, saying impatiently, 'Come in! Don't keep me waiting!'

Mr Bumble was only brave when dealing with poor, helpless people. He felt very uneasy about entering this dark building with an ill-tempered stranger. However, he was equally afraid of his wife. Nervously, he followed her through the door.

Inside, Monks stared at Mrs Bumble for some time. 'So this is the woman, is it?'

'Yes,' replied Mr Bumble cautiously.

As they walked upstairs, there was a bright flash of lightning outside, followed by loud thunder. They sat down at the table and Monks started immediately.

'So you were present when the old woman died, is that right? And she told you something?' He stared at Mrs Bumble again.

'Yes,' said Mrs Bumble. 'Something about the mother of Oliver Twist. But first, how much will you pay me for the information?'

'If it's what I want to hear – twenty-five pounds,' said Monks. 'But it's a lot of money for something which has been lying dead for twelve years.' Reluctantly, he pushed the money across the table towards her, then bent forward to listen. The faces of the three nearly touched, as the two men leant over the table to hear what the woman had to say, and the woman leant over towards them so that they could hear her whisper. In the dim lamplight their faces looked pale and ghostly.

'The old woman who was the nurse died with only me in the room,' said Mrs Bumble.

'No one else was there?' asked Monks fiercely.

'No one.'

'Good,' said Monks. 'Go on.'

'She spoke about a young woman who had given birth in the same bed some years before. The child was Oliver Twist. And this nurse had robbed the child's mother.'

'Robbed in life?' asked Monks.

'In death. She stole from the body when it was hardly cold. But the old woman fell back and died before she could tell me more.'

'It's a lie!' shouted Monks furiously. 'You know more! I'll kill you both if you don't tell me what else she said.'

'She said no more,' repeated Mrs Bumble calmly, showing (unlike Mr Bumble) no fear of the strange man's violence. 'But in her hand I found a piece of dirty paper.'

'Which contained . . .?'

'Nothing. It was only a receipt from a pawnbroker. I went to the pawnbroker and got back a little gold locket. Inside was a gold wedding ring and on the locket itself, the name "Agnes".' She put the locket on the table in front of Monks.

He picked it up immediately and looked at it closely, his hands shaking. 'Is this all?'

'It is. And now I want to ask you a question. What do you intend to do with the locket?'

'This. So it can never be used against me.' Monks suddenly pushed the table to one side and opened a small door in the floor. Down below rushed the river, its muddy waters swollen by the heavy rain.

'If you threw a man's body down there, where would it be tomorrow?' asked Monks.

'Twelve miles down the river, and cut to pieces,' replied Mr Bumble in a shaky voice.

Monks tied the locket to a heavy weight and dropped it into the water. In a second, it was gone. The three of them looked into each other's faces, and seemed to breathe more freely.

'Now we have nothing more to say,' said Monks, with a threatening look at Mr Bumble. 'And nothing to say to anyone else either. Do you understand?'

'Certainly,' said Mr Bumble, very politely. He moved away from the strange man, anxious to leave quickly.

At the door to the street, Monks turned again to Mr Bumble.

'If you threw a man's body down there, where would it be tomorrow?'
asked Monks.

'And if we ever meet again, we don't know each other. Do you understand that as well?'

'Perfectly,' said the relieved Mr Bumble, moving away into the rain and pulling his wife with him.

11

Nancy makes a visit

On the evening after the Bumbles' little business meeting, Mr Bill Sikes, waking from a sleep, called out to ask the time.

The room he was lying in was very small and dirty. It was a different room from the one he had occupied before the Chertsey expedition, but it was in the same poor part of London. There were so few possessions or comforts in the room that it was clear Mr Sikes had met hard times. He himself was thin and pale from illness, and was lying on the bed, wrapped in an old coat. The white dog lay on the floor next to him.

Seated by the window was Nancy, repairing Sikes' old jacket. She, too, was thin and pale. At Sikes' voice she raised her head from her work. 'Not long past seven,' she said. 'How do you feel now, Bill?'

'As weak as water. Help me get up, will you?'

As Nancy helped him out of bed, Sikes swore and cursed at her clumsiness. Illness had not improved his temper.

'You wouldn't speak like that if you knew how kindly I've nursed you these last few days,' said Nancy. 'So many nights, I've looked after you.' She sat down in a chair, exhausted.

'Get up!' shouted Sikes. 'What's wrong with you?'

But Nancy was unable to get up. Her head fell back against the chair and she fainted.

Sikes swore and cursed again, but Nancy remained unconscious.

'What's the matter here?' asked a voice from the door, and Fagin, followed by the Artful Dodger and Charley Bates, entered the room. When they saw Nancy, they hurried to help her. Charley rubbed her hands and the Dodger gave her a drink from the bottle he carried. Gradually, Nancy recovered her senses.

Sikes then turned to Fagin. 'What are you here for?' he asked roughly. 'You haven't been here for weeks – all the time I was ill. I haven't two coins to rub together. Why didn't you help me? You treat me worse than a dog!'

'Don't be bad-tempered, my dear,' said Fagin calmly. 'I haven't forgotten you, Bill.'

'Well, what about some money, then? I've done enough work for you recently – what about some money?'

'I haven't a single coin with me, my dear,' said Fagin.

'Then go and get some – you've got lots at home. No, I don't trust you. Nancy can go back with you to your house and fetch some money. I'll stay here and sleep.'

After a good deal of arguing, Fagin managed to reduce the amount Sikes was demanding from five pounds to three pounds. He went back to his house with Nancy and the boys.

When they were inside, Fagin told the girl, 'I'll just go upstairs and fetch the cash for Bill, my dear. There's little money in this business, Nancy, little money and no thanks – but I'm fond of seeing the young people around me.'

Suddenly there was a man's voice at the front door. As soon as Nancy heard it, she sat up in her chair.

'That's the man I was expecting earlier,' said Fagin. 'Don't worry. He'll only be ten minutes.'

The man entered the room. It was Monks. When he saw Nancy, he moved back, as if he had expected no one but Fagin.

'It's all right, only one of my young people,' Fagin said to him. 'Did you see him?'

'Yes,' answered Monks.

'Any news?'

'Good news,' said Monks with a smile. 'Let me have a word with you.' He and Fagin went upstairs to talk privately.

As soon as they had left the room, Nancy took off her shoes and crept silently up the stairs to listen in the passage – as she had done once before. She was gone for a quarter of an hour, then, like a ghost, she reappeared in the downstairs room and sat down. Immediately afterwards, the two men descended the stairs.

'How pale you are, Nancy!' said Fagin, once Monks had left the house. 'What have you been doing to yourself?'

'Nothing – except waiting here for you too long,' she answered, turning her face away from him. 'Now, where's the money for Bill?'

With a sigh for every piece of money, Fagin put the agreed amount into her hand.

When Nancy was out in the street again, she sat down on a doorstep, and for a few minutes seemed unable to move. Then she started running wildly through the streets, and when she was exhausted she stopped and burst into tears. This strange mood seemed to leave her then, and she turned and hurried back to Sikes' house.

At first when she returned, Sikes noticed nothing unusual about her. Fagin, with his sharp, suspicious eyes, would have noticed something at once. But as night came, the girl's nervous excitement increased and even Sikes was alarmed by the paleness in her cheeks and the fire in her eye.

He lay in bed, drinking hot gin-and-water, and staring at her. 'You look like a corpse that's come back to life again. What's the matter with you tonight?'

'Nothing. Why are you staring at me so hard?'

'Either you've caught the fever yourself, or – no, you're not going to . . . you wouldn't do that!'

'Do what?' asked the girl.

'There's not a girl alive as loyal as you. If you weren't, I'd have cut your throat months ago. No, you must have the fever coming on, that's it. Now, give me some of my medicine.'

Nancy quickly poured out his medicine with her back to him. He took it, and after turning restlessly for some time, he eventually fell into a deep, heavy sleep.

'The drug's taken effect at last,' Nancy said to herself as she rose from her position beside the bed. 'I hope I'm not too late.'

Quickly, she put on her coat and hat, looking round fearfully as if she expected at any moment to feel Sikes' heavy hand on her shoulder. She kissed the robber's lips softly, then ran from the house without a sound.

She hurried in the direction of west London, pushing past people on the pavement, and running across crowded streets without looking.

'The woman is mad!' said the people, turning to look at her as she rushed past them.

She came to a wealthier part of the town where the streets were quieter, and before long she had reached her destination. It was a family hotel in a quiet street near Hyde Park. The clock struck eleven as she entered.

The man at the desk looked at her and asked, 'What do you want here?'

'I want to see Miss Maylie.'

The man looked at the young woman with strong disapproval. 'She won't want to see someone like you. Come on, get out.'

'Let me see her – or two of you will have to throw me out!' said Nancy violently.

The man looked at her again, and decided it would be easier to do as she asked. He led her upstairs to Rose's room.

Nancy entered with a brave face but with fear in her heart.

'Please sit down and tell me why you wish to see me,' said Rose Maylie, looking with some surprise at this poor, rough girl from the streets. Rose's manner was so kind and sincere, and so unexpected, that Nancy burst into tears.

When she had recovered a little, she asked, 'Is the door shut?'

'Yes,' answered Rose, a little nervously. 'But why?'

'Because I am about to put my life, and the lives of others, in your hands. I am the girl that kidnapped little Oliver and took him back to old Fagin's house on the night Oliver was going to the bookseller.'

'You!' said Rose.

'Yes, it was me. I am that wicked creature you have heard about. I've no friends except thieves and robbers. I've lived on the streets since I was a child, cold, hungry, among people who are always drunk and fighting. And that's where I'll die, too.'

'I pity you!' said Rose in a broken voice.

'But I'll tell you why I'm here. Do you know a man called Monks?'

'No,' answered Rose.

'He knows you. I heard him tell Fagin that you were at this hotel. Maybe he's changed his name. Soon after Oliver was put into your house on the night of the robbery, I listened in secret to a conversation between Monks and Fagin in the dark. And I heard Monks say that he'd seen Oliver in the street, and that he knew at once Oliver was the child he was looking for, although I couldn't hear why. Monks then agreed to pay Fagin some money if he could find Oliver again, and more money if he could turn the poor boy into a thief.'

'Why?' asked Rose.

'He saw my shadow on the wall as I listened, and I had to escape. I didn't see him again until last night.'

'And what happened then?'

'I listened at the door again. And I heard Monks say this: "So the only proof of the boy's identity is at the bottom of the river, and the old woman who received it is dead." He and Fagin laughed. Then Monks said that he had all Oliver's money safely now, but how funny it would be if the boy went to prison for stealing, after his father's unfair will.'

'What *is* all this?' asked Rose.

'It's the truth, lady. Then Monks said he couldn't have Oliver killed because suspicion would point to himself. But he'd try for the rest of his life to harm the boy if he could. Then Monks laughed again about the money Oliver should have got from his father's will. "My young brother Oliver will never see that money!" he said.

'His brother!' exclaimed Rose.

'Those were his words,' said Nancy, looking round uneasily, as if she still expected to see Sikes. 'And then he talked about how amazed *you* would be if you knew who Oliver really was.'

'And this man was serious?'

'His voice was full of anger and hatred. I know many people who do worse things, but I'd rather listen to all of them than to this man Monks. But I must get back now, or people will wonder where I've been.'

'Back! How can you go back to such a life?' asked Rose. 'You've told me all this. Now I can help you by letting you stay somewhere safe.'

'No. Perhaps it's hard for you to believe, but there's one man, the most dangerous of them all, that I can never leave. You're the first person who's ever spoken to me so kindly – but it's too late.'

'It's never too late!'

'It is!' cried the girl. 'I can't leave him now. And if I tell anyone about this man, he'll die.'

'But how can I find you again, when we want to investigate this mystery further?'

'I'll meet you secretly, if you promise not to watch or follow me,' said Nancy. 'And if you promise just one more thing – not to do anything to hurt the man I can never leave.'

'I promise.'

'Every Sunday night, between eleven and twelve, I will walk on London Bridge if I am alive. Meet me there if you want more information.'

As Nancy said these words, she left the room and ran down the stairs and out into the street once more. Rose was left alone, her thoughts in great confusion, as she wondered desperately what to do and who to ask for advice.

The next morning, Oliver, who had been out walking, ran into Rose's room at the hotel. He was breathless with excitement.

'I can't believe what I've seen! Now you'll all know that I've told you the truth!' he shouted.

'I know you've always told us the truth – but what are you talking about?' asked Rose.

'I've seen Mr Brownlow, the kind man who was so good to me.'

'Where?'

'Going into a house,' said Oliver, crying with joy. 'I've got the address here.'

'Quick,' said Rose. 'Call a coach. I'll take you there immediately.'

The idea came to Rose that perhaps Mr Brownlow would advise

her. She had been afraid to tell Nancy's story to Dr Losberne, since the good doctor was very excitable and often acted with more enthusiasm than wisdom.

In less than five minutes they were in the coach on their way to the address. Rose went in first to talk to Mr Brownlow alone. She was taken into his study, and polite greetings were exchanged. When they were seated again, Rose said,

'This will surprise you very much, but you were once very kind to a dear friend of mine, and I'm sure you will be interested to hear news of him.'

'Really? May I ask you his name?'

'Oliver Twist.'

Mr Brownlow said nothing for a few seconds, but simply stared at Rose. Finally he moved his chair nearer to her and said with great feeling, 'I once thought that he was a liar and a thief. If you have evidence to show me I was wrong, please tell me at once.'

'I know him to be a child with a warm heart,' said Rose. 'And despite the hardships of his life, he's a better person than almost anyone I know.'

'I looked for him everywhere,' said Mr Brownlow, 'but I could never find him. I could never quite believe that he really did intend to rob me.'

Rose told him everything that had happened to Oliver since then. She finished by saying, 'And his only sorrow, for some months, has been that he could not find you, his former friend.'

'Thank God!' said Mr Brownlow. 'This is great happiness to me, great happiness. But why haven't you brought him with you, Miss Maylie?'

'He's waiting in a coach at the door,' replied Rose.

Mr Brownlow hurried out of the room, down the stairs and into the coach without another word. In a minute he had returned with Oliver. 'How well he looks!' he said. 'New clothes, the same sweet face, but not so pale; the same eyes, but not so sad.'

They talked with great joy for some time. Then Mr Brownlow sent for Mrs Bedwin, the old housekeeper. She came in quietly and waited for her orders.

'You get blinder every day,' said Mr Brownlow impatiently.

'People's eyes, at my time of life, don't improve with age,' replied the old lady.

'Then put on your glasses.'

As she searched for them in her pocket, Oliver could not wait any longer and ran into her arms.

'Dear God!' she said. 'It's my innocent boy!'

'My dear old nurse!' cried Oliver.

'I knew he would come back,' said the old lady, holding him in her arms. 'How well he's dressed – how well he looks again!' She laughed and cried at the same time, and could not let Oliver go.

While Oliver talked to Mrs Bedwin, Rose asked Mr Brownlow if she could speak to him privately. He led her into another room, and there listened, with a good deal of amazement, to Rose's account of her extraordinary conversation with Nancy. Between them, they decided that Mrs Maylie and Dr Losberne should be told, and that Mr Brownlow would come to the hotel that evening for a discussion. For the moment, nothing would be said to Oliver himself.

That evening at the hotel Oliver's four friends met as arranged. Dr Losberne, of course, was full of immediate plans to rush round London arresting all the gang and hanging them at once. Mr Brownlow, fortunately, was able to persuade him to abandon this wild idea.

'Then what's to be done?' cried the doctor impatiently.

'First,' said Mr Brownlow calmly, 'we must discover who Oliver's parents were. Then – if this girl's story is true – we must regain the inheritance that should have been his.'

'Yes, yes,' said the doctor, nodding in agreement. 'But how shall we achieve these aims?'

'We must find this man Monks,' said Mr Brownlow. 'Nancy will not betray the man who is special to her, but she will surely agree to tell us how or where to find Monks. Then we must find a way to force Monks to talk. We must be both cautious and clever. After all, we have no proof against him, and if we cannot make him talk, this mystery will never be solved. But we'll have to wait five days until Sunday before we can meet Nancy on London Bridge. Until then, we can do nothing.'

12

Nancy keeps an appointment

On exactly the same night as Nancy had met Rose Maylie, two people from Oliver's home town were making their way towards London. Their progress was slow, since they travelled on foot, and in addition, the girl was carrying a heavy bag on her back. The young man carried nothing. From time to time he turned to shout at the girl behind him. 'Hurry up! What a lazy creature you are, Charlotte! I'll come and give you a kick if you don't move faster!'

The young man was Noah Claypole, who had made Oliver's life so miserable at Mr Sowerberry's house. He was now taller and uglier but otherwise little changed. He and Charlotte had grown tired of the undertaking business and had set off to London to start a new life – with all the money from Mr Sowerberry's shop in their pockets.

Eventually, they entered London, and Noah began to look for a quiet, cheap pub where they could spend the night. Charlotte followed obediently at his heels as they walked through a district of narrow, dirty streets.

At last Noah found a pub that he thought was suitable. It was dark and dirty, with a few rough-looking men in the bar. They entered and asked for a room for the night and a meal of cold meat and beer, which they ate in the bar. The beer made Noah talkative and he began to boast. 'So it's no more coffins for us, my girl. We can do better than just robbing Mr Sowerberry. In London there are pockets, houses, coaches – even banks!'

'I like the sound of it, Noah, but how are we going to do all this?' asked Charlotte.

'We can meet people who know about these things. I'd like to be the leader of some gang, if there's a good profit to be made in that kind of work.' Noah felt very pleased with himself, and looked forward to an easy life of crime in the capital.

They talked about their plans for a few minutes. Then a stranger, who had been sitting unseen round the corner, came up to them. The stranger was Fagin. He greeted them in a very friendly and cheerful way, sat down with them, and immediately ordered more beer for Noah.

'That's good beer,' said Noah, already a little drunk. He thanked the stranger for the drink.

'Expensive, too,' said Fagin. 'If you drink that every day, my dear, you'll need to empty pockets, houses, coaches, even banks.'

When he heard his own words repeated, Noah went pale with

terror. The stranger must have heard everything, even how they had robbed Mr Sowerberry!

'Don't worry,' laughed Fagin, pulling his chair closer. 'You're lucky it was only me who heard you.'

'I didn't take it,' said Noah quickly. 'It was the woman who did it!'

'It doesn't matter who did it, my dear,' replied Fagin, looking quickly at Charlotte. 'Because I'm in that business myself. And the people in my house as well. I can introduce you to the right people, if you're interested. You both look like good workers.'

Charlotte and Noah felt a mixture of fear and pleasure. 'What would you want me to do?' asked Noah. 'Something light, if possible,' he added.

'What about spying on people?' asked Fagin. 'Or robbing young children who are going shopping for their mothers? That's light work, and easy.'

Noah laughed. 'That sounds like just the thing for me! And what will I earn for this work?'

'You can live free in my house, and give me half of what you earn.'

After further discussion, and the transfer of Mr Sowerberry's money from Noah's pocket to Fagin's, agreement was reached. The next day Noah and Charlotte went to live in Fagin's house and began to be instructed in their new profession.

Although training and experience had made Nancy an expert liar, she could not completely hide the fear in her mind. She knew she had taken an enormous risk in going to see Rose Maylie. If Fagin or Sikes ever found out . . . But she pushed these fears away. She was determined to keep her promise to Rose Maylie, and meet her as

After further discussion between Noah Claypole and Fagin,
agreement was reached.

arranged.

On the first Sunday night after her meeting with Rose, she was in Sikes' room when the clock struck eleven. Fagin was there, too, discussing some business with Sikes. Nancy stood up and put on her coat. Sikes watched her, surprised.

'Nancy! Where are you going at this time of night?'

'Not far.'

'What kind of answer is that? Where are you going?'

'I don't know,' replied the girl.

'Then I do. Nowhere. Sit down.'

'I'm not well. I want a breath of air.'

Sikes got up and locked the door.

'Let me go!' said the girl with great force. 'Just for one hour – let me go!'

Sikes seized her arms roughly. 'The girl's gone mad!'

Nancy fought wildly, and Sikes had to hold her down in a chair. She continued to scream and fight until midnight, when, exhausted and tearful, she stopped struggling. She went into another room and threw herself on a bed.

'She's a strange girl,' Sikes said to Fagin, shaking his head. 'Why did she suddenly decide to go out tonight? I thought that after all these years I'd finally tamed her. She must be ill – perhaps she's still got a bit of fever.'

'That must be it,' said Fagin, nodding thoughtfully.

As he walked home, Fagin's eyes were sharp with suspicion. He had suspected for a while that Nancy had become tired of Bill Sikes' brutality and violence, and that she had found a new friend to take his place. Her manner was different; she often left home alone, and she seemed less interested in the gang. And tonight, her desperate impatience to go out at a particular hour . . . He was certain he was right. He began to make plans.

First, he wanted to know who Nancy's new friend was. He could make him a valuable new member of the gang, with Nancy as his assistant. But there was another, darker reason. Fagin, too, had become tired of Sikes. Sikes knew too much – too many dangerous secrets about Fagin himself. Fagin distrusted everybody, but he hated and distrusted Sikes most of all. It would be very convenient if Sikes could be . . . removed.

'With a little persuasion,' Fagin thought, 'perhaps the girl would poison Sikes.' Suddenly, his eyes narrowed in delight. 'Yes! First, I must have her watched, and find out who her new man is. Then I shall threaten to tell Sikes everything. She knows that neither she nor her new man will ever be safe from Sikes' violent jealousy. She will have no choice except to do as I ask her – and then, once the murder is done, she will be in my power for ever!'

Early next morning Fagin called the newest member of his gang. Noah was doing very well. He had already brought home quite a lot of money. He had found that robbing small children was indeed light, easy work, and he was proud of his success.

'I have another job for you now,' Fagin told him. 'It needs great care and secrecy. I want you to follow a woman. I want to know where she goes, who she sees, and if possible, what she says. I will pay you a pound for this information.'

Noah's eyes were wide with greed. 'I'm the right man for this job. Who is she?'

'One of us.'

'What? You don't trust her, then?'

'Exactly so, my dear. Exactly so,' smiled Fagin.

The following Sunday, soon after eleven o'clock, a woman walked quickly through the dark streets towards London Bridge. A mist hung over the river, and the buildings on the far bank could hardly be seen. A man followed some distance behind her, keeping to the darkest shadows. It was a cold, damp night, and there were very few people on the streets at this late hour.

When the woman reached the centre of the bridge, she stopped and looked around anxiously. The man following her stopped too. The heavy bell of St Paul's cathedral rang out, announcing the death of another day. Just as it finished, a grey-haired man and a young woman got out of a coach and walked across the bridge. They met the woman, who took them down some steps leading to the river bank. They stood in deep shadow by the wall of the bridge. The man hurried down some other steps, crept up to the corner of the wall, and listened.

Nancy spoke first. 'I'm so frightened tonight I can hardly breathe.'

'Frightened of what?' asked Mr Brownlow. He seemed to pity her.

'I wish I knew. Horrible thoughts of death, and blood, have been with me all day. I don't know why.'

'Speak to her kindly,' said Rose to Mr Brownlow. 'Poor girl! She seems to need it.'

'I couldn't come last Sunday,' continued the girl. 'I was kept in by force. But tonight he'll be out all night until daylight. Now, before I tell you anything else, I must tell you that I don't want Fagin, or any of the other members of the gang, to be handed to the police.'

'Why not?'

'Because I couldn't betray them. They've been loyal to me, and I'll stay loyal to them.'

'Then just tell us how we can get Monks, and I promise none of your friends will be harmed,' said Mr Brownlow.

'And Monks will never know how you found out about him?' she asked.

'We promise,' said Rose gently.

Nancy then told them, in so low a voice that the listener round

The man crept up to the corner of the wall, and listened.

the corner could hardly hear her, where Monks often went for a drink, and what he looked like. She finished by saying, 'On his throat, high up, there is —'

'A bright red mark?' asked Mr Brownlow.

83

'Do you know him?' asked Nancy in surprise.

'I think I do.' Mr Brownlow murmured to himself, 'It must be him!' Then more loudly, he said to Nancy, 'Thank you for everything you've told us. But now – how can you go back to these people? Come with us now, tonight. We can arrange for you to be hidden from them all forever, if you want us to.'

The girl shook her head. 'I'm chained to them, bad as they are. I've gone too far to change my life now.' She looked nervously over her shoulder. 'I can feel those dreadful terrors again – visions of blood and death. I must go home.'

Mr Brownlow and Rose could not persuade her to change her mind. Sadly, they turned to leave, and when they had gone, Nancy fell to the ground in a storm of tears. Meanwhile, Noah Claypole, amazed by all that he had heard, crept up the steps and ran for Fagin's house as fast as his legs could carry him.

Some hours later, nearly two hours before dawn, Noah lay asleep in Fagin's house. But Fagin sat silently by a dead fire, staring at the flame of a candle on the table beside him. With his pale, wrinkled face and his red, staring eyes, he looked like a devil out of hell. Hatred ran like poison through his every thought. Hatred for the girl who had dared to talk to strangers, who had ruined his plan to get rid of Sikes. He did not believe her promise not to betray him, and he feared that he would now be caught, and hanged.

Just before dawn Sikes entered the room, carrying a bundle which contained the results of his night's work. Fagin took what Sikes gave him, then stared at the robber for a long time without speaking.

'Why are you looking at me like that?' asked Sikes, uneasy at the old man's strange expression.

Fagin raised his hand, but his passion was so great that he could not speak.

'Say something, will you!' shouted Sikes, placing his huge hand on Fagin's collar and shaking him in his anger and fear. 'Open your mouth and say what you've got to say!'

Eventually Fagin found his voice. 'Bill, what would you do if one of the gang went out at night and told someone all about us, and what we'd done? What would you do to him?'

'I'd smash his head into little pieces,' said the robber, swearing violently.

'And what if it was me, who knows so much about all of us, and could put us all in prison and get us all hanged?' whispered Fagin, his eyes flashing with hate.

'I'd beat your brains out in public. Even in the law-court, I'd run over and kill you with my bare hands,' said Sikes, showing his teeth in his anger. 'I don't care who it was, that's what I'd do.'

Fagin woke Noah. 'Tell Bill what you told me, what you saw, what she did. Tell him!'

Noah rubbed the sleep from his eyes and told Sikes everything. His face white with passion, Sikes listened to the end, then, swearing furiously, he rushed from the room and down the stairs.

'Bill!' Fagin called after him. 'You won't be . . . too violent?'

Sikes made no reply, but, pulling open the door, ran out into the silent streets. He did not turn his head to right or left, but looked straight in front of him with wild determination. He ran at great speed, his eyes on fire, his teeth tight together, and did not pause until he reached his own door. He ran up to his room, entered and locked the door, put a table against it, then woke Nancy.

'Bill!' she said, pleased to see him. But when she saw his

expression, the colour went out of her face. 'What's the matter?' she said in alarm.

'You know what.' Sikes took out his gun, but realizing, even in his madness, that a shot might be heard, he beat her twice across the face with it as hard as he could. She fell, with a low cry of pain and terror, almost blinded by the blood that flowed from the cut on her forehead. The murderer staggered to a corner, seized a heavy stick and struck her down.

13

The end of the gang

The sun burst upon the crowded city in all its brightness. It lit up every corner of London, the great houses of the rich, and the miserable homes of the poor. It shone everywhere, even into the room where the murdered woman lay. The horror of that scene was even more dreadful in the clear morning light.

Sikes sat there, unable to move, looking at the body. He had thrown the blood-covered stick into the fire, then washed himself and his clothes. He had cut out the bits of his clothes that were stained and burnt them too, but there were still bloodstains all over the floor. Even the dog's feet were bloody.

Finally, he forced himself to leave the room, pulling the dog out with him and locking the door behind him. He walked rapidly north, towards Highgate, then on to Hampstead. On the open land of Hampstead Heath, away from people and houses, he found a place in a field where he could sleep without being disturbed.

But before long he was up again and running. This time he ran back towards London for a while. Then he turned and went north again, sometimes walking, sometimes running, with no clear purpose in his mind. Eventually, he felt hungry, and changed direction towards Hendon, a quiet place away from the crowds, where he could buy food. But even the children and chickens there seemed to look at him with suspicion. So he turned back towards Hampstead Heath again, without having eaten, uncertain where to go.

At last he turned north again, his dog still running at his heels, and set off to a village just outside London. He stopped at a small, quiet pub and bought a meal, then went on again. It was now dark and as he continued walking, he felt as if Nancy were following him, her shadow on the road, her last low cry in the wind. If he stopped, the ghostly figure did the same. If he ran, it ran too, moving stiffly, like a corpse. Sometimes he turned, determined to drive the ghost away, but his blood ran cold with terror. Every time he turned, the ghost turned too, and was still behind him.

Finally, he found another field where he could hide. He lay down, unable to sleep, his mind filled with visions of the dead girl. Her wide, dead eyes stared at him, watching him through a curtain of blood.

Suddenly he heard shouting in the distance. He jumped to his feet and saw that the sky seemed on fire. Sheets of flame shot into the air, driving clouds of smoke in his direction. He heard an alarm bell, and more shouts of 'Fire!' Running with his dog across the fields, he joined the crowds of men and women fighting the fire. He could forget his own terror in this new danger, and he worked all night with the crowd, shouting, running and working together to stop the flames destroying more buildings.

In the morning the mad excitement was over, and the dreadful memory of his crime returned – more terrifying than ever. In desperation, he decided to go back to London.

'At least there'll be somebody I can speak to,' he thought to himself. 'And it's a better hiding-place than out here in the country. I'll hide there for a week, get some money out of Fagin, then escape to France.'

Suddenly he remembered the dog – people would be looking for his dog as well as himself. He decided to drown the animal. But the dog smelt the man's fear, and turned and ran away from him faster than it had ever run in its life.

'You have a choice, Mr Monks,' said Mr Brownlow. 'You have been kidnapped and brought here to my house. You can either tell me what I want to know, or I'll have you arrested, instantly, for fraud and robbery. It's your choice. And you must decide now. At once.'

Monks hesitated and looked at the old man, but Mr Brownlow's expression was so serious and determined that the younger man realized it was pointless to protest. 'I didn't expect this treatment from my father's oldest friend,' said Monks angrily, sitting down with a frown on his face.

'Yes, I was your father's oldest friend,' said Mr Brownlow. 'And I know all about you – how your father, while still a boy, was forced by his family into an unhappy marriage with an older woman, and how you were the result of that marriage. I also know that your parents separated, hating each other by the end.'

'Well – what's so important about that?'

'When they'd been separated for ten years,' said Mr Brownlow, 'your father met another family. There were two daughters, one nineteen years old and the other only two or three. Your father

Sikes decided to drown his dog.

became engaged to the older daughter. At this point one of his rich relations died and left him a lot of money in his will. Your father had to travel to Italy to receive his inheritance, and while there, he became ill and died. Your mother, who was living with you in Paris, immediately rushed to Italy when she heard the news. As your father had made no will of his own, all the relation's money came to you and her.'

Monks listened with close attention, biting his lip and staring at the floor.

'Before your father went to receive that money, he came to see me,' continued Mr Brownlow slowly, his eyes fixed on Monks' face.

'I never heard that before,' said Monks, looking up suddenly, a suspicious expression on his face.

'He left me a picture of the poor girl he wanted to marry. He talked wildly about shame and guilt, and how he would give part of the money he'd inherited to his wife and to you, and use the rest to escape from England with the girl he loved. He refused to tell me any more details.'

Monks breathed more easily, and even smiled.

'But,' said Mr Brownlow, pulling his chair nearer to the other man, 'by chance I was able to rescue your brother Oliver from a life of misery and — '

'What!' cried Monks.

Mr Brownlow continued without a pause. 'And when he was recovering from his sickness here in my house, I noticed how similar he looked to the girl's face in the picture. But he was taken away before I could discover his history – as you know very well.'

'You can't prove anything!' said Monks.

'I can. I heard that you were in the West Indies. I went there to try and find you to see if you knew anything about Oliver, but you'd already left. I returned to London, and was unable to find you until two hours ago.'

'And now what? You can't prove that Oliver's my brother.' Monks smiled unpleasantly.

'I couldn't before,' said Mr Brownlow, standing up. 'But now I can. There was a will, but your mother destroyed it. This will mentioned a child that would be born later; this was Oliver, the child you met later by accident. You noticed his resemblance to your father and you became suspicious. You then went back to his birthplace, found proof of his birth and the fact that he's your half-brother, and destroyed that proof.'

Monks sat in silence, his eyes filled with fear.

'Yes,' continued Mr Brownlow fiercely, 'shadows on the wall have caught your whispers with Fagin, and brought them to my ear. For the sake of that innocent child, whom you wanted to destroy. And now murder has been done, and you are as guilty of that as if you had struck the blow yourself!'

'No, no,' said Monks quickly. 'I knew nothing of that. Nothing at all.' He was silent for a while, realizing how much was known about him. Hatred and fear fought inside him, but he was a coward at heart. At last, seeing no escape, he raised his head. 'I will admit everything – in front of witnesses, if necessary.'

Mr Brownlow nodded coldly. 'I will prepare a document for you to sign. You must give Oliver what is really his, and then you can go where you please.'

At that moment Dr Losberne rushed into the room. 'The murderer will be taken tonight! His dog's been found.'

'And Fagin?' asked Mr Brownlow.

'They're sure of him. They may have him already.'

Mr Brownlow turned back to Monks. 'Have you made up your mind?'

'Yes,' replied Monks. 'And you promise – it'll remain a secret?

No police, or charges of fraud against me?'

'Yes,' said Mr Brownlow. 'You have my promise. For now, you must remain here, locked in this room. I will come for you tomorrow evening and take you to sign a confession in front of witnesses.'

Mr Brownlow then left the room with the doctor, and they eagerly discussed the news of the hunt for the criminals. 'My blood boils with anger,' said Mr Brownlow. 'This poor murdered girl must be revenged. You stay here and guard Monks. I'll go out and get the latest news.'

The two men parted, each in a fever of excitement.

Down by the river Thames was a district called Rotherhithe, one of the dirtiest and roughest places in London. The houses next to the river had no owners; they were broken down and ruined, but could be defended against attack. In an upper room of one of these houses, were three members of Fagin's gang.

'When was Fagin taken, then?' asked the man called Toby.

'Two o'clock this afternoon. Charley and I escaped up the chimney, but Noah was caught. Bet went to see Nancy and when she saw the body, she started screaming and wouldn't stop. She's been taken to hospital.'

'What's happened to Charley Bates?'

'He'll come here when it's dark. It's too dangerous now.'

'We're in trouble,' said Toby. 'Fagin's going to hang – that's certain.'

'You should have seen him when he was caught,' said another robber. 'The police carried him through the crowd while all the people jumped at him, screaming and trying to attack him.'

Suddenly Sikes' dog ran into the room. All the robbers rushed out immediately to look for Sikes, but there was no sign of him. They returned to the upstairs room.

'I hope he's not coming here,' said Toby.

'The dog's come a long way,' said another man. 'Covered in mud, and tired out.'

They sat there in silence, wondering where Sikes was. It was already dark when they heard a sudden, hurried knock at the door downstairs.

Toby went to the window to look down, then pulled his head back in, his face pale with fear. There was no need to tell the others who it was.

'We must let him in,' said Toby, although none of them wanted to see him. Toby went down to the door and returned, followed by Sikes. White-faced, with a three-day-old beard, hollow cheeks and staring eyes, Sikes looked like a ghost. No one said a word.

'Nothing to say to me?' Sikes asked.

The only answer was a low shout of many voices from outside in the distance, coming closer. Lights appeared. Looking out, Sikes saw a stream of people crossing the bridge towards them. Then there was a loud knocking on the door and more shouts from the crowd.

'The doors are made of metal and they're locked and chained,' said Toby. The three robbers watched Sikes nervously, as if he were a wild animal.

'Bring a ladder!' shouted some of the crowd below.

'Give me a rope, quick,' Sikes said to the others. 'I'll go the other way, climb down the back and escape over the river. Get me a rope – now! Or I'll do three more murders!'

A minute later, Sikes appeared on the roof and the shouts from the crowd below swelled to a great roar. Then the front door was smashed down and people streamed into the house. Sikes quickly tied the rope around the chimney, then began to tie the other end around himself, ready to lower himself to the ground behind the house. But just as he put the rope over his head, he screamed in

Sikes quickly tied the rope around the chimney.

terror and threw his arms above his head. He staggered back, slipped and fell over the edge of the roof. As he fell, the rope tightened around his neck with a horrible jerk. In a second the murderer was dead, and there he hung, his body swinging gently from side to side. The dog, which had followed its master onto the roof, jumped down towards the lifeless body, missed, and fell dead on the stones below.

14

The end of the mystery

The next day Oliver travelled with Mr Brownlow, Dr Losberne, Mrs Maylie and Rose back to his birthplace. He had been told a little of his history, and knew that there would be more explanations at the end of this journey. He was anxious and uncertain, wondering what he would hear.

But towards the end of the journey, he began to recognize familiar places, and in great excitement pointed them out to Rose. There was the path he had taken when he had run away. There, across the fields, was the 'baby farm'. Then, as they drove into the town, he saw the house of Mr Sowerberry the undertaker, and the workhouse that had been his prison.

They stopped at the biggest hotel in the town, and went in to their rooms. During dinner Mr Brownlow stayed in a separate room, and the older members of the group went in and out with serious faces. Mrs Maylie came back with her eyes red from crying. All this made Rose and Oliver, who had not been told any new secrets, very nervous and uncomfortable.

At nine o'clock Dr Losberne and Mr Brownlow brought Monks

into the room. Oliver was very surprised; this was the same man he had bumped into once outside a pub, and seen another time with Fagin, looking in at him through the window of the country cottage. Oliver was told that Monks was his half-brother, and the boy stared at him in shock and amazement. Monks looked back at him with hatred.

'We have the whole story here in these papers,' said Mr Brownlow, putting them on the table. 'All we need now is for you to sign them, Monks. And to tell Oliver what happened.'

Monks started hesitantly. 'My father had arrived in Italy to collect the money he had inherited, when suddenly he fell ill. When he died, we found two papers in his desk. One was a letter to his girl; the other was a will.'

'What was the letter?' asked Mr Brownlow.

'It was written when he was ill, telling the girl how ashamed he was that she was pregnant. He asked her not to remember him as a bad man but as someone who had made a mistake. He reminded her of the day he'd given her the locket and ring.'

Oliver's tears fell fast as he listened to the story of his father.

'And what about the will?' asked Mr Brownlow.

Monks was silent.

'The will', continued Mr Brownlow, speaking for him, 'was in the same spirit as the letter. He talked of the misery of his marriage to his wife, and the evil character of you, Monks, his only son, who had been brought up by your mother to hate him. He left you and your mother an annual income of £800. The rest of his property he left to his girl Agnes and to their child, if it were born alive, and if it showed itself to be of a good, kind character. The money would only go to you, Monks, as the older son, if the younger turned out to be as evil as you.'

'My mother', said Monks, 'burnt this will, and never sent the letter. The girl Agnes left her home in secret, so that her pregnancy would not bring shame on her family. I swore to my mother, when she was dying, that if I ever found my half-brother, I would do him all the harm I could. He would feel my hatred like a whip on his back. I paid Fagin to trap Oliver into a life of crime. But then he escaped, and that stupid, interfering girl Nancy talked to you. If I'd had the chance, I would have finished what I'd begun.' Monks stared at Oliver, and his lips moved in a silent curse.

'And the locket and ring?' asked Mr Brownlow.

'I bought them from Mr and Mrs Bumble, who had stolen them from the nurse, who had stolen them from Agnes, the dead girl. I've already told you how I threw them into the river.'

Mr Brownlow turned to Rose. 'I have one more thing to explain,' he said to the girl.

'I don't know if I have the strength to hear it now,' she murmured, 'having heard so much already.'

Mr Brownlow put his hand under her arm. 'You have a great deal of courage, dear child,' he said kindly. He turned to Monks. 'Do you know this young lady, sir?'

'Yes.'

'I don't know you,' said Rose faintly.

'The father of poor Agnes had *two* daughters,' said Mr Brownlow. 'What happened to the other one, who was only a young child at the time?'

'When Agnes disappeared,' replied Monks, 'her father changed his name and moved to a lonely place in Wales, where no one would know about the family shame. He died very soon afterwards, and this young daughter was taken in by some poor people. My mother hated Agnes and everybody connected with her. She hunted for this

97

young sister, and made sure that her life would be unhappy. She told the poor people who had taken her in that the girl was illegitimate, and that she came from a bad family with an evil reputation. So the child led a life of miserable poverty – until Mrs Maylie saw her by chance, pitied her, and took her home.'

'And do you see this young sister now?' asked Mr Brownlow.

'Yes. Standing by your side.'

Rose could hardly speak. 'So . . . Oliver is my nephew?'

'I can never call you aunt,' cried Oliver. 'You'll always be my own dear sister!'

They ran into each other's arms, both of them crying in their happiness. A father, sister and mother had been lost and gained, and it was too much for one evening. They stood for a long time in silence, and the others left them alone.

The court was full of faces; from every corner, all eyes were on one man – Fagin. In front of him, behind, above, below – he seemed surrounded by staring eyes. Not one of the faces showed any sympathy towards him; all were determined that he should hang. At last, there was a cry of 'Silence!', and everyone looked towards the door. The jury returned, and passed close to Fagin. He could tell nothing from their faces; they could have been made of stone. Then there was complete stillness – not a whisper, not a breath . . . Guilty. The whole court rang with a great shout, echoing through all the rooms as the crowd ran out of the building to tell all the people waiting outside. The news was that he would die on Monday.

Fagin thought of nothing but death that night. He began to remember all the people he had ever known who had been hanged. He could hardly count them. They might have sat in the same prison cell as he was now. He thought about death by hanging –

the rope, the cloth bag over the head, the sudden change from strong men to bundles of clothes, hanging at the end of a rope.

As his last night came, despair seized Fagin's evil soul. He could

As his last night came, despair seized Fagin's evil soul.

not sit still, and hurried up and down his small cell, gasping with terror, his eyes flashing with hate and anger. Then he lay trembling on his stone bed and listened to the clock striking the hours. Where would he be when those hours came round again?

In the middle of that Sunday night, Mr Brownlow and Oliver were allowed to enter the prison. Several strong doors were unlocked, and eventually they entered Fagin's cell. The old robber was sitting on the bed, whispering to himself, his face more like a trapped animal's than a human's.

'You have some papers, Fagin,' said Mr Brownlow quietly, 'which were given to you by Monks to look after.'

'It's a lie!' replied Fagin, not looking at him. 'I haven't got any.'

'For the love of God,' said Mr Brownlow, very seriously, 'don't lie to us now, on the night before your death. You know that Sikes is dead and Monks has confessed. Where are the papers?'

'I'll tell you, Oliver,' said Fagin. 'Come here.' He whispered to him. 'They're in a bag up the chimney in the front room at the top of the house. But I want to talk to you, my dear.'

'Yes,' said Oliver. 'Will you pray with me?'

'Outside, outside,' said Fagin, pushing the boy in front of him towards the door. 'Say I've gone to sleep – they'll believe *you*. You can take me out with you when you go.' The old man's eyes shone with a mad light.

'It's no good,' said Mr Brownlow, taking Oliver's hand. 'He's gone too far, and we can never reach him now.'

The cell door opened, and as the visitors left, Fagin started struggling and fighting with his guards, screaming so loudly that the prison walls rang with the sound.

They left the prison building in the grey light of dawn. Outside in the street, huge crowds were already gathering, joking and laughing, and pushing to get the best places near the great black platform, where the rope hung ready for its morning's work.

Less than three months later, Rose married Harry Maylie. For her sake, Harry had abandoned his political ambitions, and had become a simple man of the church. There was no longer any mystery about Rose's birth, but even if there had been, Harry would not have cared. They lived next to the church in a peaceful village. Mrs Maylie went to live with them, and spent the rest of her days in quiet contentment.

Mr Brownlow adopted Oliver as his son. They moved to a house in the same quiet village, and were just as happy. Dr Losberne discovered suddenly that the air in Chertsey did not suit him. In less than three months he, too, had moved – to a cottage just outside the village, where he took up gardening and fishing with great energy and enthusiasm.

Mr Brownlow suggested that half the remaining money from the will should be given to Monks and the other half to Oliver, although by law it should all have gone to Oliver alone. Oliver was glad to accept the suggestion. Monks went off with his money to the other side of the world, where he spent it quickly and was soon in prison for another act of fraud. In prison he became ill and died. The remaining members of Fagin's gang died in similar ways in other distant countries, all except Charley Bates, who turned his back on his past life of crime and lived honestly, as a farmer.

Noah Claypole was given a free pardon for telling the police about Fagin. He soon became employed as an informer for the police, spying on people and telling the police about anyone who had broken the law. Mr and Mrs Bumble lost their jobs and became poorer and poorer, eventually living in poverty in the same workhouse that they had once managed.

In that quiet country village, the years passed peacefully. Mr Brownlow filled the mind of his adopted son with knowledge, and as he watched the boy grow up, he was reminded more and more of his old friend, Oliver's father. The two orphans, Rose and Oliver, led lives that were truly happy. The hardships that they had once suffered had left no bitterness in their gentle souls, and all their lives they showed the mercy and kindness to others that God himself shows to all things that breathe.

GLOSSARY

beadle a kind of former police officer who dealt with the poor
   people of a town or country district
career a person's working life and its progress or development
cart a simple uncovered carriage, pulled by a horse
cell a small room for one or more prisoners in a prison
charity (school) a free school for poor children, paid for by rich
   people
coach (in this story) a large four-wheeled carriage pulled by
   horses
coffin a wooden box in which a dead person is buried
commit (a crime) to do something illegal or wrong
corpse a dead body
dawn *(n)* the time of day when light first appears
devil a very wicked person, or Satan, the enemy of God; also used
   for emphasis in questions, e.g. *What the devil are you doing?*
dim (of a light) faint, not bright
drunk/drunken confused, helpless, violent, etc. because of
   drinking too much alcohol
evil *(adj)* very bad, wicked
fit *(n)* a sudden attack of a disease which causes violent
   movements and loss of consciousness
fraud deceiving somebody illegally in order to make money or
   obtain possessions
furious full of violent anger
gentleman a man of good family, usually wealthy
gin a strong, colourless alcoholic drink
handkerchief a small piece of cloth for wiping the nose or eyes

hang to kill somebody by hanging them from a rope around the
  neck, as a legal punishment for a crime
housekeeper a person employed to manage a house and do the
  housework
identity who a person is
illegitimate born of parents who are not married to each other
inheritance money, possessions, etc. received as a result of the
  death of the previous owner
jerk *(n)* a very sudden, sharp movement
kidnap *(v)* to steal somebody away by force and keep him/her a
  prisoner illegally
lean *(v)* to bend, to be in a sloping position
locket a small ornamental case, worn on a chain around the neck
magistrate a judge who deals with smaller crimes in local courts
master *(n)* a male employer, the man in control
mouse a small animal with a long tail, found in houses or fields
orphan a child whose parents are dead
passion strong deep feeling, of hate, love, or anger
pawnbroker a person who lends money in exchange for valuable
  things left with him, which he can sell later if the money is not
  repaid
poverty the state of being poor
rat an animal similar to a mouse, but larger
reluctant unwilling and therefore slow to agree, act, etc.
resemblance similarity, looking like something or somebody else
roar *(n and v)* a long loud deep sound, like that made by a lion
ruin *(v)* to damage badly or destroy
seize to take hold of suddenly and violently
servant someone employed to do work in a house
spirit a person's mind and emotions, often their courage or
  liveliness

stagger *(v)* to walk or move unsteadily as if about to fall

stick *(v)* to put or fix something in a position or place

strike *(v)* to hit somebody violently; also, to show the time by sounding a bell in a clock

swing *(v)* to move backwards and forwards while hanging or supported

take up to begin doing something (e.g. a hobby) regularly

undertaker a person whose business is to prepare the dead for burial and arrange funerals

will *(n)* a legal document which states what somebody wants to happen to their money and property after their death

workhouse in former times, a place provided by the government for the very poor, where they were fed and housed in exchange for work done

Before Reading

1 **Read the story introduction on the first page, and the back cover. What do you know now about the people in this story? Circle Y (Yes) or N (No) for each sentence.**

  1 Oliver Twist's parents are still alive. Y/N
  2 Oliver is poor and homeless. Y/N
  3 Fagin and Bill Sikes are wicked criminals. Y/N
  4 The Artful Dodger and Charley Bates are honest boys, and are
     kind to Oliver. Y/N
  5 Nancy's situation is a difficult and unpleasant one. Y/N

2 **What do you think is going to happen to the people in this story? Choose the most probable of these ideas.**

  Oliver Twist
  1 He becomes a hardened criminal like the others.
  2 He persuades his new friends to give up playing their 'games'.
  3 He makes other friends, who help him lead a good, happy life.
  Bill Sikes and Fagin
  4 They both die in the end.
  5 One of them is hanged for his crimes, and the other escapes.
  6 One of them kills the other.
  Nancy
  7 She betrays her friends in the end.
  8 She is murdered.
  9 She finds happiness in the end.

While Reading

Read Chapters 1 to 4. Who said this, and to whom? Who or what were they talking about?

1 'Let me see the child, and die.'
2 'The old story.'
3 'I don't like to see them suffer.'
4 'Please, sir, I want some more.'
5 'You see if I'm not right.'
6 'Why shouldn't I be able to make use of them in my work?'
7 'Everybody hates me.'
8 'You'll sleep here, among the coffins!'
9 'She was so bad it was lucky she died.'
10 'It's the meat that's caused this, you know.'
11 'We've just taken them all out to wash them, that's all!'
12 'What fine men they were! Loyal to the end.'
13 'Do you see that old man outside the bookshop? He's the one.'
14 'I'm afraid he's hurt himself.'

Before you read Chapter 5 (*Oliver's life changes*), can you guess the answers to these questions?

1 Will Oliver be sent to prison?
2 Will the old gentleman try to help him?
3 Will the Dodger and Charley Bates rescue him?
4 Will the policeman believe Oliver and let him go?
5 Will Oliver ever return to Fagin's house?

Read Chapters 5 to 8. Choose the best question-word for these questions, and then answer them.

What / Who / Why

1 . . . was Mr Brownlow reluctant to take Oliver to court?
2 . . . was the magistrate in court that day, and . . . was he like?
3 . . . had seen Mr Brownlow's handkerchief being stolen?
4 . . . were Fagin and Bill Sikes worried about Oliver's arrest?
5 . . . did Nancy pretend to be at the police station?
6 . . . did Mr Brownlow and Mr Grimwig disagree about?
7 . . . kidnapped Oliver and took him back to Fagin's house?
8 . . . was Mr Bumble's reward for his information about Oliver?
9 . . . did Fagin want Oliver to 'do the job' at Chertsey?
10 . . . did the dying nurse in the workhouse tell Mrs Corney?
11 . . . did the stranger called Monks want Fagin to do to Oliver?
12 . . . happened after Oliver was shot and Sikes pulled him out?
13 . . . did the servants find on the front doorstep the next day?

Before you read Chapter 9 (*Oliver starts another life*), can you guess what happens? Circle Y (Yes) or N (No) for each idea.

1 Oliver is arrested and sent to prison for attempted burglary. Y/N
2 His new life is considerably worse than his past life. Y/N
3 The young lady takes pity on him and befriends him. Y/N

Read Chapters 9 to 11. Are these questions true (T) or false (F)? Rewrite the false sentences with the correct information.

1 Rose was Mrs Maylie's daughter.
2 Dr Losberne failed to persuade Mrs Maylie's servants that Oliver was not one of the burglars.

3 Oliver was unable to prove his honesty to Mr Brownlow.
4 Harry Maylie did not want to marry Rose because of her doubtful birth.
5 Fagin met Mr Bumble in a pub and sold him some information.
6 Monks threw Agnes' locket into the river.
7 Nancy listened to two conversations between Fagin and Monks.
8 Monks had taken money that Rose should have inherited.
9 Nancy made Rose promise that Bill Sikes would be arrested.

Before you read Chapter 12 (*Nancy keeps an appointment*), can you guess the answers to these questions?

1 Will Bill Sikes or Fagin begin to be suspicious of Nancy?
2 Will Mr Brownlow find Monks and make him tell the truth?
3 Will Oliver receive his rightful inheritance?

Read Chapters 12 to 14, and answer these questions.

1 How did Fagin persuade Noah and Charlotte to join his gang?
2 Why did Fagin suspect Nancy of having a new lover?
3 Why did Nancy want to prevent the gang from being punished?
4 How could Monks easily be identified?
5 What was the chain of events that led to Nancy's murder?
6 How did Bill Sikes die?
7 What relation was Monks to Oliver?
8 What happened to the will that Oliver's father had left?
9 Why did Monks want to trap Oliver into a life of crime?
10 What relation was Rose to Oliver?
11 What happened to the money that Monks had inherited?
12 Which members of Fagin's gang did not die in prison?

After Reading

1 **Which characters are thinking these thoughts, and who or what are they thinking about? Explain what the thoughts tell us about these characters. Then put them in the correct order, as they would occur in the story.**

1 'She's tired of him. She's been behaving strangely for a while now. Look how desperate she was to go out at eleven tonight. She's found someone to replace him – I'm certain of it.'

2 'Stupid of me! I should have realized what the old gentleman wanted to hear about that boy. If only I'd told him Oliver was honest and good! I would have got another ten pounds then!'

3 'Poor girl! I pity her so much. How can she live such a life, with that awful gang of robbers? She seemed so frightened of them. Next time I see her, I must persuade her to escape from them.'

4 'My new friend has been very good to me. I think I'd have died of hunger if he hadn't bought me some food. He says he'll help me find somewhere to live in London. It's lucky I met him.'

5 'That mean old devil treats me like a dog! Why hasn't he been to see me since I've been ill? Next time he comes, he'd better give me some money, or I'll smash his head against the wall!'

6 'I've seen some horrible crimes committed, but making that innocent child into a criminal is going too far. I've got to stop Monks and Fagin, but how? Yes! I'll go and find this Rose Maylie now, at once, and warn her . . .'

7 'Dear Miss Maylie! I simply cannot resist a pretty woman in tears! I'm sure I can shake the servants' belief that this boy was one of the burglars. A few fierce questions, plenty of beer . . .'

8 'Could that poor little boy really have stolen my handkerchief? He's got an honest-looking face. And I'm afraid he was hurt in the chase. No, I really don't want him punished.'

2 **What did Mr Brownlow and Mr Grimwig say when Oliver did not return from the bookseller? (See page 34.) Complete Mr Brownlow's side of the conversation.**

MR GRIMWIG: You see, Brownlow? I told you so!

MR BROWNLOW: _____

MR GRIMWIG: Impatient? We've already waited half an hour. The bookshop's only just round the corner!

MR BROWNLOW: _____

MR GRIMWIG: I don't think so! You can go to the hospital and ask there, if you like, but you'll be wasting your time!

MR BROWNLOW: _____

MR GRIMWIG: Why would anyone want to kidnap him? No, I'm sorry, my old friend. That boy is just a common thief.

MR BROWNLOW: _____

MR GRIMWIG: He can, and he is. He deceived you very cleverly.

MR BROWNLOW: _____

MR GRIMWIG: He certainly looked sweet and innocent, I agree. But that's how he tricked you!

MR BROWNLOW: _____

MR GRIMWIG: I'm sure of it. At this moment they'll all be sharing out the clothes and money you gave him, and laughing at you!

3 Here is a newspaper report about the break-up of Fagin's gang. Put the parts of sentences in the right order, starting with number 3. Then join them with these linking words to make a paragraph of seven sentences.

after / and / but / However / that / where / which / while / who

1 _____ he accidentally hanged himself

2 _____, one of the robbers has now given information about many of the gang's crimes,

3 Yesterday police managed to arrest almost all the members of a much-feared gang of robbers,

4 _____ being arrested at the Rotherhithe house.

5 _____ is expected to hang for his crimes.

6 including the brutal murder of a young woman last Tuesday,

7 _____ have stolen large amounts of money and valuables.

8 Other members of the gang were taken to prison to await trial,

9 For years the police have been trying to catch him and his gang,

10 _____ the murderer was the young woman's lover, a gang member called Bill Sikes.

11 _____ until now they have not been able to collect enough evidence to convict them.

12 _____ has shocked the whole of London.

13 _____ trying to escape from the crowd pursuing him.

14 Sikes was eventually trapped in a ruined house at Rotherhithe,

15 Police believe, from information received,

16 The gang-leader, a man called Fagin, was caught at his home at two o'clock in the afternoon,

4 **Now choose the best headline to go with the newspaper report.**

ARRESTS AT ROTHERHITHE   CAUGHT AT LAST!

INFORMER HELPS POLICE   GANG-LEADER TO HANG

FAGIN FINISHED!   FAGIN'S GANG ARRESTED

5 **Perhaps Mrs Maylie wrote to Harry, telling him what Mr Brownlow had discovered. Complete the letter with the right characters' names, or with one suitable word for other gaps.**

My dear Harry,

I have some most exciting _____ to tell you! It concerns the young _____ boy, _____. Our good, kind friend, _____, has discovered a lot more about his family. Apparently, Oliver's father did not get on well with his wife, and _____ from her. Their son was called _____. After ten years of separation, Oliver's father fell in love with a sweet girl called _____, and gave her a wedding ring and a gold _____ as _____ of his love. Just before he died, he discovered she was _____, and left most of his money to her in his _____. Monks' mother found this _____ and burnt it, so that she and her son could _____ all the money, and Monks later found and destroyed the ring and locket. Poor Agnes died in the _____, giving birth to a son. It was the beadle, _____, who gave him the name of Oliver Twist. I am really _____ for little Oliver! Now he will have half his father's _____, and will never live in _____ again.

But we also learnt that poor Agnes had a younger _____, and that sister is _____! So she is not _____. Her parents were highly _____ people, and she no longer needs to be _____ of her birth. So perhaps, dear Harry, she will give you a _____ answer now.

    Your loving Mother

6 Here are Mr Grimwig and Mr Brownlow again, at the end of the story. Complete Mr Grimwig's side of the conversation.

MR BROWNLOW: Well, Grimwig, you were wrong about young Oliver, weren't you? Come now, admit it!

MR GRIMWIG: _____

MR BROWNLOW: But that was because he was kidnapped!

MR GRIMWIG: _____

MR BROWNLOW: I'm going to adopt him as my son.

MR GRIMWIG: _____

MR BROWNLOW: No, in the country – close to the Maylies' house.

MR GRIMWIG: _____

MR BROWNLOW: Of course, Grimwig. You'll always be welcome.

7 Think about or discuss your answers to these questions. Give reasons for your opinions.

1 Do you think Nancy betrayed her friends? What would *you* have done? Is it ever right to reveal your friends' secrets to other people, or is loyalty more important than anything else?

2 Did Monks deserve half his father's money? Why do you think Mr Brownlow suggested this course of action? Would it have been better for Oliver to give Monks's share to charity?

3 Noah Claypole was given a free pardon for telling the police about Fagin. Was this right? Or should informers who are criminals also be punished?

4 Bill Sikes beat Nancy to death, but was Fagin equally guilty of this murder? Why, or why not?

5 Fagin was hanged for his crimes. Is it right for the state to put a convicted criminal to death? If so, for which crimes?

ABOUT THE AUTHOR

Charles John Huffam Dickens (1812–70) was born in Portsmouth, a port in the south of England. His father was a clerk in the Royal Navy pay office, a well-meaning but irresponsible man, and very bad at managing money. Dickens spent some happy childhood years in Kent, but when the family moved to London, their money problems resulted in his father's imprisonment for debt in the Marshalsea prison, and at the age of twelve Dickens was sent to work in a factory. Bitter memories of this deeply unhappy time influenced much of his writing. Later, he was able to return to school for a few years, and after a time as an office boy, he became a journalist, writing for various newspapers. In these early years Dickens got to know London extremely well – all its highways and passages, its squares and markets and gardens, and this was knowledge that he put to very good use in his novels.

In 1836 he married Catherine Hogarth, and in the same year his first novel, *The Pickwick Papers*, began to appear in monthly instalments in a magazine. This was very popular, and was soon followed by *Oliver Twist* and several more novels. They were all written as serials for monthly magazines, and published as books later. Readers eagerly greeted each new novel, and Dickens quickly became both successful and wealthy.

As well as his writing, Dickens found time for a busy social life with his large family and wide circle of friends, for his theatrical activities, for editing magazines, and for travelling in America and Europe. He also had a great interest in the social problems of the times – a concern that appears in many of his novels. For example, in his famous story *A Christmas Carol* (1843), Scrooge is shown as mean and hard-hearted because he refuses to give money to the hungry and the homeless.

As he grew older, Dickens worked harder than ever, and the novels of these later years – *Dombey and Son, David Copperfield, Bleak House, Hard Times, Little Dorrit, A Tale of Two Cities, Great Expectations* – are often considered to be his finest works. His personal life, though, became rather difficult, and his marriage came to an end when he and Catherine separated in 1858. The novels, however, continued to appear, and Dickens toured Britain and the United States, giving public readings from his works. It was a very full but also exhausting life, and in 1870, at the age of 58, Dickens died suddenly, leaving unfinished his last novel, *The Mystery of Edwin Drood*.

Oliver Twist was published in 1838. 'I have thrown my whole heart and soul into Oliver,' Dickens wrote. His aims were to show, in little Oliver, how goodness can triumph over evil, and to show the criminal underworld in all its 'miserable reality'. He also makes a fierce attack on the New Poor Law of 1834, which provided relief for the poor only in workhouses, where conditions were deliberately harsh. But for Dickens, the heart of the novel was Nancy. 'I mean to do great things with Nancy,' he wrote, and in her he combined his two aims of showing criminals 'as they really are', and the 'principle of Good surviving through every adverse circumstance'.

There have been many film and stage adaptations of Dickens's novels, including a popular musical of *Oliver Twist*. Dickens is often called the greatest English novelist of all time, and his characters and their sayings have become so real to us that they are now part of our language and our everyday life.

ABOUT BOOKWORMS

OXFORD BOOKWORMS LIBRARY
Classics • True Stories • Fantasy & Horror • Human Interest
Crime & Mystery • Thriller & Adventure

The OXFORD BOOKWORMS LIBRARY offers a wide range of original and adapted stories, both classic and modern, which take learners from elementary to advanced level through six carefully graded language stages:

Stage 1 (400 headwords)	**Stage 4** (1400 headwords)
Stage 2 (700 headwords)	**Stage 5** (1800 headwords)
Stage 3 (1000 headwords)	**Stage 6** (2500 headwords)

More than fifty titles are also available on cassette, and there are many titles at Stages 1 to 4 which are specially recommended for younger learners. In addition to the introductions and activities in each Bookworm, resource material includes photocopiable test worksheets and Teacher's Handbooks, which contain advice on running a class library and using cassettes, and the answers for the activities in the books.

Several other series are linked to the OXFORD BOOKWORMS LIBRARY. They range from highly illustrated readers for young learners, to playscripts, non-fiction readers, and unsimplified texts for advanced learners.

Oxford Bookworms Starters *Oxford Bookworms Factfiles*
Oxford Bookworms Playscripts *Oxford Bookworms Collection*

Details of these series and a full list of all titles in the OXFORD BOOKWORMS LIBRARY can be found in the *Oxford English* catalogues. A selection of titles from the OXFORD BOOKWORMS LIBRARY can be found on the next pages.

BOOKWORMS • CLASSICS • STAGE 5

David Copperfield

CHARLES DICKENS

Retold by Clare West

'Please, Mr Murdstone! Don't beat me! I've tried to learn my lessons, really I have, sir!' sobs David.

Although he is only eight years old, Mr Murdstone does beat him, and David is so frightened that he bites his cruel stepfather's hand. For that, he is kept locked in his room for five days and nights, and nobody is allowed to speak to him.

As David grows up, he learns that life is full of trouble and misery and cruelty. But he also finds laughter and kindness, trust and friendship . . . and love.

BOOKWORMS • CLASSICS • STAGE 6

Jane Eyre

CHARLOTTE BRONTË

Retold by Clare West

Jane Eyre is alone in the world. Disliked by her aunt's family, she is sent away to school. Here she learns that a young girl, with neither money nor family to support her, can expect little from the world. She survives, but she wants more from life than simply to survive: she wants respect, and love. When she goes to work for Mr Rochester, she hopes she has found both at once. But the sound of strange laughter, late at night, behind a locked door, warns her that her troubles are only beginning.

Pride and Prejudice

JANE AUSTEN

Retold by Clare West

'The moment I first met you, I noticed your pride, your sense of superiority, and your selfish disdain for the feelings of others. You are the last man in the world whom I could ever be persuaded to marry,' said Elizabeth Bennet.

And so Elizabeth rejects the proud Mr Darcy. Can nothing overcome her prejudice against him? And what of the other Bennet girls – their fortunes, and misfortunes, in the business of getting husbands?

This famous novel by Jane Austen is full of wise and humorous observation of the people and manners of her times.

Tess of the d'Urbervilles

THOMAS HARDY

Retold by Clare West

A pretty young girl has to leave home to make money for her family. She is clever and a good worker; but she is uneducated and does not know the cruel ways of the world. So, when a rich young man says he loves her, she is careful – but not careful enough. He is persuasive, and she is overwhelmed. It is not her fault, but the world says it is. Her young life is already stained by men's desires, and by death.

Dublin People

MAEVE BINCHY

Retold by Jennifer Bassett

A young country girl comes to live and work in Dublin. Jo is determined to be modern and independent, and to have a wonderful time. But life in a big city is full of strange surprises for a shy country girl . . .

Gerry Moore is a man with a problem – alcohol. He knows he must give it up, and his family and friends watch nervously as he battles against it. But drink is a hard enemy to fight . . .

These stories by the Irish writer Maeve Binchy are full of affectionate humour and wit, and sometimes a little sadness.

OXFORD BOOKWORMS COLLECTION

Fiction by well-known authors, both classic and modern.
Texts are not abridged or simplified in any way, but have
notes and questions to help the reader.

From the Cradle to the Grave

Short stories by

EVELYN WAUGH, SOMERSET MAUGHAM, ROALD DAHL, SAKI,
FRANK SARGESON, RAYMOND CARVER, H. E. BATES, SUSAN HILL

This collection of short stories explores the trials of life from youth to old age: the idealism of young people, the stresses of marriage, the anxieties of parenthood, and the loneliness and fears of older people. There is a wide variety of styles of writing, from black humour and satire to compassionate and realistic observation of the follies and foibles of humankind.